Engaging
Jesus
with Our
Senses

Engaging Jesus with Our Senses

AN EMBODIED APPROACH
TO THE GOSPELS

JEANNINE MARIE HANGER

Baker Academic
a division of Baker Publishing Group
Grand Rapids, Michigan

Published by Baker Academic
a division of Baker Publishing Group
Grand Rapids, Michigan
BakerAcademic.com

Printed in the United States of America

Library of Congress Cataloging-in-Publication Data
Names: Hanger, Jeannine Marie, author.
Title: Engaging Jesus with our senses : an embodied approach to the Gospels / Jeannine Marie Hanger.
Description: Grand Rapids, Michigan : Baker Academic, a division of Baker Publishing Group, [2024] | Includes bibliographical references and index.
Identifiers: LCCN 2023053566 | ISBN 9781540966728 (paperback) | ISBN 9781540968302 (casebound) | ISBN 9781493447534 (ebook) | ISBN 9781493447541 (pdf)
Subjects: LCSH: Senses and sensation—Religious aspects—Christianity. | Bible. Gospels. | Jesus Christ.
Classification: LCC BT741.3 .H365 2024 | DDC 261.5/15—dc23/eng/20240124
LC record available at https://lccn.loc.gov/2023053566

Cover design by Paula Gibson
Cover art: Mosaic of Mary Magdalene and Christ (artist unknown) / 3LH-Fine Art / Superstock

Baker Publishing Group publications use paper produced from sustainable forestry practices and postconsumer waste whenever possible.

24 25 26 27 28 29 30   7 6 5 4 3 2 1

To Garrick,
who selflessly lightens my load
and has made my dreams his own.
You are the embodiment
of the grace of Christ in my life.
I love you.

Contents

Foreword

GRANT MACASKILL

Taste and see that the LORD is good;
    blessed is the one who takes refuge in him.
                           —Psalm 34:8

Some things are better felt than telt.[1]
                  —Scots traditional saying

A few years ago, when I was in my late forties, I was diagnosed as autistic. The diagnosis didn't come out of the blue, and the long process of reaching it made sense of a lot of things in my life. It explained why my experience of sensory stimuli was so different from that of people around me—why things that smelled nice to others were actually painful to me, why I heard sounds persistently that others didn't even notice, why some sudden noises could be processed as a visual flash—and it also explained why I often thought differently than people around me did. I had grown up with a kind of sensory saturation that most others hadn't experienced, and it had affected the way that my mind developed and the way I thought about the world. I sensed the world differently, and that affected my whole way

---

1. "Telt" = "telled," i.e., told, spoken or explained.

of *being* in the world. This has a lot of relevance to my evaluation of Jeannine's book and why I think an awareness of the senses is so important to how we read the Bible in the modern world and how we think about participating in the life of God. Let me explain.

Research into sensory processing, often informed by autism, has highlighted that what we consider to be the "objective" external world, perceived through the senses, is actually a heavily filtered interpretation of sensory data, with the construct often looking quite different for neurodivergent people. In the past, sensory factors were often treated as if they were a kind of odd side effect of autism, but more recent research has moved them into the center of the conversation, recognizing that some of the distinctive features of autistic thinking may reflect the distinctive features of autistic sensing, the different "sensorium" of the autistic person.

This reflects a growing awareness in some research that human cognition—the way we think about things—is always "embodied," involving our physical senses and the processes of sense making by which we interpret what they tell us. This "embodied cognition," moreover, is not just a feature of the individual person's relationship to the world, as if that individual is a self-contained knower, because our bodies and senses participate in a social world, in communities. What I just referred to as a "growing awareness" of embodied cognition in modern research is actually a kind of retrieval, a recovery of something that was (and is) widely acknowledged by thinkers outside of the modern West or the Global North and is still often affirmed in minority cultures. For various reasons, though, it has been widely lost in the dominant intellectual frameworks of the West.

When we talk about what it means to "know" or "understand" something, particularly in the modern West or Global North, we often identify the process we describe purely in terms of what is going on in our brains, or in the intellectual processes that happen within them. More than we typically recognize, this is a legacy of modern philosophical developments that valorize something called "rationality" and the principles of logic that supposedly align with it, isolating both (sometimes quite deliberately) from the web of other realities that might legitimately inform our perception and evaluation of the world in which we exist. Some have described this way of thinking as "hypercognitive," but "hypercranial" might be a better way of labelling it; for, as Jeannine will highlight in this book, we should properly understand the entirety of our bodies and the full range of our senses to be involved in our cognitive processing. The problem with modern Western and Northern values is not so much that they are obsessed with cognition, but that they tend to consider cognition to be a process that primarily happens in the bit of an individual person that is located in their cranium.

Thinking in this hypercranial way about "thinking" itself, or about "knowing," does two things that are especially problematic for Christian discipleship, because they make "knowing God" something we mainly do with our brains and not our bodies.

First, it loses sight of the complex and dynamic ways that our senses and our bodies inform our knowledge of the world and our decision-making within it. This is not simply about the data that our senses mediate, moment by moment, but also about how those data are ordered and how the sensory "picture" that emerges comes to shape language itself, wired into the grammars and idioms that we use every day without pausing to think about how sensual they are. Have I argued "clearly" or "unclearly"? Is my logic "sharp" or "blunt"? Am I "winsome" or "obnoxious"? Here, we are using sensory terms to comprehend or communicate the properties of something that is not itself perceptible to the physical senses: an idea, an argument, an attitude. Our sensory experiences inform the way we understand and talk about higher order things that transcend the world of the senses, and this involves remapping sensory language onto realities that are relational rather than simply physical: love, for example, is *warm*, but rage is *hot*. We use this kind of language tacitly, instinctively, because it allows us to communicate something that is otherwise intangible. Understanding this allows us to be more mindful of the world around us, and also to be more mindful of our own practices of speech, including those we use in our God-talk, our theology. How do we use sensory language to talk responsibly about a God who is beyond the senses? How does the incarnation, the taking of a sensory and sensible form by that God, affect this?

Second, it loses sight (oops . . . another sensory idiom!) of the dynamic and participatory involvement of the knower with the world that they are making sense of. Think, for a moment, of how you know what water is. You probably know what it is—what its properties are—because you have drunk it, felt cooled and refreshed by it, but also because you have washed in it and been cleansed by it, or perhaps have swum in it. I do a lot of swimming, just as Jeannine does a lot of running, and I know what it is to feel water yield as a liquid to the hand that enters at the correct angle and then give the right sort of resistance to the palm that pulls then pushes back on it, sculling slightly to catch as much as possible and project the body forward. I know what water *is* because I know what it feels like, and I know what it feels like by being in it or taking it into myself. In certain regards, our knowing of the water in these experiences is not "objective" but "participatory": we are interacting with the water, being changed or moved by it. Any swimmer will tell you that the key to swimming well is working with the water; any thirsty person will tell you that the key to recovery is to take the properties of the water into yourself. And all of this is before we even talk about how beautiful it can be, when we look on water as a loch (you will possibly say "lake") or as a sea. You can label water H_2O and thereby describe its composition, but you have hardly come to *know* water by doing this. To know water truly involves gratitude for the whole range of ways in which it can drench our senses and vivify our bodies.

These analogical and participatory aspects of sensory knowledge are at the heart of what Jeannine explores in this book. For one thing, our participatory knowledge of earthly things like water and food provides sensory analogies to what it might mean to participate in the life of God through Christ and the Spirit. We are, after all, enjoined to "taste and see that the LORD is good" (Ps. 34:8). If we know what it is to be quenched, fed, or cleansed with earthly things, then we have categories that allow us to understand what it is like to be fulfilled and purified by Jesus and the Spirit. For another thing, this under-standing of participation is nourished and enabled by the bodily and sensory practices that are built into liturgy and sacrament: there is something about breaking then eating bread and about drinking wine that communicates a truth beyond words. Communication here is about not just the articulation of propositions but the sharing of some quality or reality with another.

Jeannine's book explores the ways that the New Testament writers represent salvation, and the sin from which we are saved, as something sensory and sensual. For these writers, our participation in God and in the world that God has made involves the senses, in ways that we may not be adequately mindful of as we read them today. Studying the New Testament in a way that is attentive to its sensory content is more challenging than we may expect: we have to ensure that our own senses appropriately feed into our imagination, as we read the texts in question and pick up on their sensory cues, but we also have to be aware that there are different sensory cultures. The way we talk about the senses, even the list of things that we label as "senses," is quite different in modern Western societies, especially urban ones, from in other cultures past and present. While she was working on her doctoral thesis, which concerned sensory elements in John's Gospel, Jeannine and I talked about the fact that I was familiar with the smell of death and decay, because I had grown up in a rural world of subsistence-level farming, where we often came across dead animals. That is one illustration of cultural difference, between those in rural and those in urban environments, the latter generally removed from agricultural experience. But there are all kinds of ways in which the rural culture I grew up in is also different from the east Mediterranean and west Asian culture of the New Testament world, which have their own sensorium. We need to do some hard work with "sensory anthropology" if we are to read the New Testament well.

Thankfully, Jeannine has done that work, and the result is an enjoyable and accessible introduction to the sensory qualities of the New Testament writings. I hope that all who read it will find themselves thinking in fresh ways about what it means to participate in God and the world, as their sensory neurons fire and rewire. For the salvation described in the New Testament involves the redemption of our bodies through God's incarnation in the body of Jesus Christ.

Acknowledgments

In many ways I think of this book as an extension of my doctoral studies, which focused on the sensory elements of the "I am" sayings in the Gospel of John. At the very same time, parts of this book represent the seeds of that research. May God be praised—I am constantly in wonder at this sensory life in all its colorful, fragrant, delicious, melodic glory.

There are many people to thank. First, I owe much of the shape of this study to the amazing Anna Gissing, my editor at Baker Academic. From the idea stage to the editing process, when she took time to comb through and provide feedback on every chapter, she has been incredible to work with. Thank you, Anna, for encouraging me from start to finish! Thank you also to the fantastic team at Baker Academic, including James Korsmo and Anna English, as well as to the careful and insightful freelance editor and proofreaders, for all your work on this labor of love.

I was first introduced to Anna Gissing by Carmen Imes, my colleague at Biola University who has also become a dear friend. Thanks, Carmen, for generously sharing your wisdom about publishing, writing, and more. I am inspired by your integrity and your zeal for this wonderful job we get to do! Additional friends and colleagues at Biola continually encourage me in my writing, teaching, and life balance (goals). Thank you especially to Charlie Trimm for your friendship and for reading early drafts of the bread chapter. Thank you to my deans, Doug Huffman and Scott Rae, and to my undergrad New Testament colleagues, including Joanne Jung, Darian Lockett, Jon Lunde, Ken Berding, James Petitfils, Michelle Lee-Barnewall, Jeanette Pifer, and Matt Williams. A shout-out also extends to my fellow "podcasters" on the South Bay shuttle (Brandon Cash, James P.). I am *so* grateful to work alongside such godly, wise, and uplifting people!

I am grateful to my Gospel of John students at Biola during the 2022–23 school year. They were my test case for the formational exercises appearing at the end of each chapter. I enjoyed reading their sharpening reflections and witnessing the light bulbs go on because of the memorable, affective connections that our senses create when we study Scripture.

Gratitude extends to my doctoral adviser, Grant Macaskill, who encouraged me to not shy away from the different research question (which this was). Thank you for writing the foreword to this book. I am also thankful for my dear friends in the trenches of research, who have also been a helpful sounding board for several chapters: Lisa Igram and Melissa Tan. What would I do without your collaboration and wisdom?

I wrote this book over a period of five months this year, and during this time there were friends who sustained me with coffee, meals, encouragement, and fun. There are too many to name here, but I do want to specifically thank Meredith and Joe Lopez, Melinda and Shawn Hurley, Nikki Hernandez, my Community Group, and my Indigo gals. I love you all dearly. I am thankful for my Coastline Covenant Church family and its leadership. Several of you have sacrificed to create space for a voice like mine, and this encouragement has fueled my confidence for a writing endeavor like this. Thanks especially to Garrick, Shawn, and Andrew Faris.

I am grateful for my extended Pera family, who furnished the nostalgic sensory memories in this book. Thank you also to my parents, Robert and Donna Pera; to my parents-in-law, Dwight and Vicki Hanger; and to my siblings Julie, Stephanie, and Joseph, and their families. Goodness, where would I be without you all? Your love has sustained me through the years. To my kids, Bella, Emery, and Garrison: I know you must be weary of my incessant work this summer, all to write a "Jesus book." Your humor, your love for me, and your patience have meant the world.

Finally, I have to shout my gratitude from the rooftops for Garrick, to whom this book is dedicated. God must really love me to pair me with someone as awesome as you! I know I'm not always easy to live with. Thanks for calming my anxieties, for being kinder to me than I am to myself, and for sacrificing downtime together so that I could get all these words out on paper. I love you and I love getting to do this life together.

Introduction

Why the Physical Senses Matter
for Reading Texts

"C'mon, Jeannine, let's say it again."

My mind was blank. "Chris, I don't know if I can." My friend was trying to distract me. Trying to get me to think of anything else but the sweltering heat.

"You can. Let's try to remember." He started, "Therefore, since we are surrounded by such a great cloud of witnesses . . ." Our feet kept pounding the pavement. The crowds were lined up on both sides of the street, cheering.

I was trying to remember. "Let us throw off everything that hinders . . ." I shuddered at the chills coursing through my body. Heat exhaustion was setting in. My mind was fuzzy. I wanted to stop.

". . . let us run the race marked out for us." We were attempting to run our first-ever marathon. But the heat was sweltering.

"Look, a water station!" We grasped at the cups of water handed out by volunteers. I took one to drink, one to pour over my head. It revived me enough to keep moving.

I was a freshman in college that year. Chris was dating one of my closest friends, and a large group of us had road-tripped down from Santa Barbara to Los Angeles so that three of us could accomplish this exciting goal. We had done our training. We had carbo-loaded

1

the night before. And we were the epitome of fresh-faced, idealistic Christian youth: in anticipation of the marathon, we had eagerly decided to memorize a biblical text. Thinking we were so novel, we settled on what turned out to be every runner's favorite: Hebrews 12:1–3. It's a passage all about endurance in the life of faith, pictured as a great race: *Therefore, since we are surrounded by such a great cloud of witnesses, let us throw off everything that hinders, and the sin that so easily entangles, and let us run with perseverance the race marked out for us. Let us fix our eyes on Jesus, the author and perfecter of our faith, who for the joy set before him endured the cross, scorning its shame, and sat down at the right hand of the throne of God. Consider him who endures such opposition from sinful men, so that you will not grow weary and lose heart.*[1] It seemed perfectly appropriate for the event.

So we thought we were prepared to run the 26.2 miles in every way, but no one had anticipated the heat. That early March Sunday was unseasonably warm, and it was the hottest marathon day Los Angeles had ever seen—just our luck. We had been barely eight miles in when we witnessed the third of our trio require medical attention due to the heat. After bidding farewell to the ambulance, we continued on—shaken and far too exhausted for how much we still had to go.

As we slowly wound our way through the racecourse, I was not at all sure how much longer I could make it. I began to take in water at every mile where volunteers offered it. Evidently, the race organizers had not anticipated the heat either, and when the cups of water were gone, city workers opened up fire hydrants. The water absolutely revived me. I both drank it and let it douse me whenever possible.

The second dynamic that sustained me throughout the course was the encouragement provided by the crowds. Their cheering, their clapping, and their excitement were contagious. It pushed me along with all the other runners. As the fever chills began to dissipate, I began to cast off my introverted shyness and lean into the encouragement. I began to crave it. The crowd embodied the "cloud of witnesses" of Hebrews 12:1, and soon I began to participate in the high fives

---

1. This is the 1984 version of the NIV. Italics in Scripture quotations have been added for emphasis.

being offered. I spent the better part of fifteen miles taking in water whenever I could and literally high-fiving my way to the finish line. Contrary to what you might think, this excruciating event did not prompt me to quit running—just the opposite. This experience became a building block in what has become a lifelong daily routine. Running, for me, has come to have a regulatory effect on my physical health, my mental and emotional rhythms, and my spiritual life with God. The reason I tell this story, however, is because of a tactile habit I've developed quite by accident. Over time, I realized that it traces back to that scorching day in Los Angeles. For years and years, on any given morning run, whenever I pass an eye-level species of palm tree—which are multitudinous in Southern California—I reach out and brush its fronds with my hand. I came to notice how every time I brush a palm branch it reminds me of the "cloud of witnesses" in Hebrews 12. I couldn't figure out this connection until I realized what I was doing: I was "high-fiving" the branches. This tactile action somehow puts me right back on the marathon course, imbibing whatever encouragement I can on that day—it reminds me of the people cheering me to keep on going despite the heat, despite the exhaustion. Unthinkingly, I had transferred these tactile memories into an embodied practice in my current running life. Today, on a run, when I am thinking, or praying, or reflecting on life, I can "high-five" a branch and immediately recall in my body a memory of being encouraged, of being lifted up by others. This simple gesture never fails to remind me that I am not alone in this life. It gives me a boost and helps me get through whatever I am currently going through. I marvel at how the body holds memories that can influence us today and that can help shape us going forward.

What This Book Is About

This is a book about the physical senses. As described in this funny little tale of my own sensory life, many of us have memories, emotions, and experiences embedded in the depths of our embodied lives. It is through our sensory faculties that we experience the world. These sensory abilities have the power to encode all kinds of experiences into the fabric of our beings, including the extremes—from compassion and peace to trauma and violence. Our sensory abilities also have the capacity to recall these very same experiences, reflections, and emotions. All of this suggests that our physical senses *matter* to how we walk through this life. Thus, to a certain degree this book highlights the role of the senses in our lives.

But this is also a book about engaging biblical texts and doing so with our senses intact. That is, we are going to consider our embodied, sensory lives and ask, Do the physical senses matter to how we engage the Bible? As you might guess, the short answer is yes, the senses do matter to this endeavor. What follows is an invitation to consider why and how this is. It's an invitation to approach the biblical text with our senses. We will consider how those within the narrative perceived the world, and we will reflect on how the earliest readers might have interacted with these stories. Finally, we will land on how as readers today we can engage these stories with our senses and why this might matter to our spiritual formation. Ultimately, the following is an invitation to bring our whole sensory selves into our reading of the Gospels, seeking to understand more of God along the way.

We all lead diverse sensory lives. As we will see throughout this book, there are many ways cultures and individuals measure these diversities, and some senses are more influential on daily life than others. Moreover, we often come to realize how much we value our physical senses when one of them drops out. This realization can come as simply as when the electricity goes out at night or when someone forgets to unmute themselves on a Zoom call; or it can be more life-altering and disorienting, such as in an acute loss of a sensory ability. In many cases the level of interruption depends on how highly a given culture values certain senses.

But why bring up this sensory life in the first place? At the heart of this book is the conviction that our embodied, sensory lives reflect the creativity and beauty of God himself. And as we are gifted with varying abilities to sense the world—to see, feel, hear, smell, taste, speak, and move—I am convinced that if we pay attention, there is a way to harness these abilities toward experiencing *more* of God's goodness. More specifically, this book suggests ways we can bring our entire embodied selves into our engagement with God through his

Word, and through this to live out in a more fully embodied way the psalmist's invitation to "taste and see that the LORD is good" (Ps. 34:8).

Sensing the Good Life

"God saw all that he had made, and it was very good" (Gen. 1:31a). For those who believe that we are participants in God's good, created order, part of how we purposefully understand this goodness is through our senses. We come to understand the goodness of God by touching the soft fur of a kitten, by tasting the sweetness of a luscious berry, or by hearing the melodic song of a bird. Our senses help us to experience the goodness of this world in a fully embodied way. Thus, we can know the beauty and magnificence of God's creation with our bodies through a variety of sensory modes. If this is true, then does it follow to say that our sensory capacities matter to how we engage with God? That is, if God has created us to be in relationship with him, if we are invited to love him with our hearts, souls, minds, and strength, then this must be nothing less than engaging our entire embodied selves, including our sensory lives, in this endeavor.

But here is the problem: we often limit ourselves to engaging God through a text. Surely, the revelation of God as expressed in words—what we refer to as *the Word*—is critical. But is this revelation merely a collection of words on a page, accessed only by sight when we read them or by hearing them when they are spoken? Is there more? If words on a page articulate a world that mirrors our own—narratives about sights, sounds, smells, tastes, and touch—is there a way our sensory lives can access this sensory life on a page? Is there more to understand about the goodness of God when we bring our embodied, sensory existence to the sensory words (and worlds) in a text? I believe that there *is* more, and this study suggests ways we can bring our embodiment into our approach to *the Word*. But where in the *Word* can we begin?

Abiding in Christ has historically been a compelling theme for the church. It speaks to a quality of "with-ness" that believers have with Jesus, providing encouragement and comfort in a fallen, fractured world where sometimes God seems absent. John's scene of abiding in the vine is a go-to passage for understanding this participatory theme

(John 15:1–17), but this imagery is not the last word on the matter, since it resides within a more expansive, corporeal portrait of Jesus, the Word made flesh. All four Gospel narratives animate the works and words of Jesus using multisensory language, each contributing to a vivid portrait of believers' relationship with him.[2] This book seeks to draw attention to these embodied qualities by conducting a sensory reading of select Gospel passages.

This approach will take what is tangible in our worlds—our sensory experiences—and harness them toward two goals. First, our sensory knowledge will provide an entry into exploring the sensory world of the Gospel narratives as understood by ancient readers. Second, these sensory findings will in turn resonate back onto our sensory worlds, giving us a more embodied understanding of the text. In this way, the goal is to bring our good, sensory lives into conversation with our approach of a good God and Jesus, the Word made flesh.

Structure of This Study

What value might there be in a study focused on the sensory aspects of the Gospels? And how will we go about doing this? The following lays out an outline of the chapters you will encounter in this book.

The first two chapters play an orienting role to our approach. In chapter 1, I trace how post-Enlightenment dynamics have tended to outcast embodiment and the physical senses from the conversation about knowledge and how meaning is made. Is knowledge purely rational, or are there things we can only know through our embodied, sensory experience? We will look at recent research that demonstrates how our embodiment *is* integral to meaning and understanding. From here we will survey the various physical senses featured in this book, along with the history of how they have been valued.

This will lead us to discuss the *how* of our approach. How can we meaningfully engage with the senses in the biblical text? How can we bridge the mind-body divide through an open awareness of the

---

2. For example, a wonderful study that lays out the sensory aspects of the Gospel of John is Lee, "Gospel of John and the Five Senses."

senses? I suggest that imagination plays a fundamental role in our comprehension of narrative. Now, if thinking about imagination in relation to engaging a biblical text makes you nervous, this is where I hope to remove the suspicions and stigmas attached to it. Finally, I will discuss the convergence of the senses, imagination, and memory. By this I hope to set up a scaffolding that can help us understand *how* imagination operates in our method.

In chapter 2, I introduce our approach to the Gospels more specifically, with several specific points of discussion. First, I orient us to the Gospels themselves. Why are there four? How do they relate to one another, and why address the Synoptic Gospels (Matthew, Mark, Luke) and then John? I will also clarify the audiences and readers we will be addressing throughout the book. When engaging a Gospel narrative, each audience/reader represents a distinct perspective. This includes the narrative audience, ancient readers, and modern readers. We will also explore the concept of the "ideal reader" of a text, which in the case of the Gospels corresponds to readers who respond in belief. In other words, for Gospel writers, the *ideal* is that readers will be receptive to their presentation of the life, death, and resurrection of Jesus Christ. Second, we will look at the sensory quality of many of Jesus's invitations to potential disciples within the narrative. This discussion helps lay the groundwork for our approach to the Synoptics and John. Finally, I will present a brief survey of how the Holy Spirit features throughout the Gospels. Since we are seeking a fuller understanding of believers' abiding life with Christ, it is important to understand how this union is actualized by the indwelling Holy Spirit, enabling the very readers of the Gospels to comprehend the implications of the texts we will explore.

The five chapters to follow are ordered around the five physical senses that are the most resonant both in the biblical texts and in our modern sensory contexts: taste, sight, hearing, smell, touch.[3] I also would like to clarify that the senses don't always fall into separate categories of experience. As you might *sense*, we live multisensory and what many refer to as "synaesthetic" lives; that is, we experience

---

3. Modern Western sensory hierarchies tend to prioritize sight and hearing, followed by smell, taste, then touch. Rather than follow this order, we are going to begin with a lower-ranked sense: taste.

our sensory lives in overlapping ways, using multiple senses at once. Tastes come with smells, and many sights have sounds attached to them. In focusing on one sense at a time, I do not deny that other senses are also firing simultaneously. I will nuance these discussions as much as possible.

Each sensory chapter follows a similar outline. After a brief introduction, I will present insights on that chapter's physical sense. From here we will survey its presence in the Synoptic Gospels. Matthew, Mark, and Luke are grouped together because of their frequently paralleled, overlapping passages. I will call attention to relevant sensory differences across similar passages, and I will also highlight sensory scenes that might not be represented by all three of these Gospels. After this we will turn to John, commonly referred to as the Fourth Gospel. The sensory elements in John are slightly different. Many that we will survey are connected to Jesus's words and statements about himself, and these will sometimes converge with his works.

After surveying the Gospel texts, I will discuss the response of the earliest (ancient) readers, distinguishing pertinent differences between Jewish and gentile reception of these words. This will be followed by reflections on the sensory implications for modern readers, you and me. At the end of each chapter, I provide a list of exercises inviting further reflection on the topic at hand. Each one is an opportunity for you to engage your own physical senses as part of this reflection. This will help you get beyond just reading a text, asking God to meet you as you seek to more fully "digest" his words, so to speak. I hope that you enjoy these.

In the final chapter, I present some concluding reflections. Here I will pull together the threads that were woven through our sensory survey of the Gospels. In the end, I hope that you, the reader, will have engaged the text in a fresh way and that in doing so you will have gained new insights about what it means to abide with Christ. Together, I hope that we will have tuned our senses more closely to what it means to live "the good life" in relation to God, and that we will use these reflections to take advantage of every day we've got. Now, I invite you to join me as we cleanse our palates, open our eyes, tune our ears, take a deep breath, and step into the endeavor of engaging Jesus with our senses.

1

Our Sensory Approach

Reading with Our Senses Intact

Have you ever tried to give instructions to someone and words failed to fully capture it? Instead, you resorted to saying, "Here, let me show you." Or have you ever tried to learn a skill by either listening to instructions or watching someone else engage in the activity? Take, for example, learning how to snowboard or how to ride a bike. I'll bet you didn't actually *learn* these activities until you clicked into the bindings and tried to slide your way down the mountain or until you actually pedaled the bicycle and balanced your way down the street. Notice how our embodiment is relevant to learning these skills—in these examples you engage touch and proprioception to gain knowledge. If our physical senses are relevant for learning skills like snowboarding or riding a bike, how might they figure in when engaging with a text?

The Problem: We've Lost Our Senses

Obviously, we engage our minds when reading a text, but is our embodiment at all involved in this endeavor, or has it gone missing?

9

I don't deny the importance of the mind for comprehending a text, but I wonder if we have lost how the physical senses are wrapped up into activities of the mind. The physical senses are endemic to how we as embodied creatures experience the world, and yet we often take a mental, epistemic approach to "knowledge," which tends to separate and even elevate mind over body. It has not always been this way. The following will briefly consider our tendencies to overlook the physical senses, the reasons for this, and why it might be important to integrate the physical senses more fully into the conversation about knowledge.

This mind-body gap is often traced back to the Cartesian *cogito*— "I think, therefore I am"—which has had quite a bit of influence on the popular intellectual landscape. Descartes's dictum suggests that the one thing we can know for sure is *that* we exist as thinking beings; we are distinct because of our rationality. In the wake of this view the body came to be understood as being somewhat unrelated to the human capacity for reasoning. This ultimately led to "a basic ontological gulf between mind and body, reason and sensation."[1] Kantian thought endeavored to explain this gap but ultimately upheld this mind-body dichotomy.[2]

This mind-body divide has been seen as a bridge to additional dualisms, pitting not only the cognitive against the embodied but also the conceptual against the perceptual, objective against subjective, knowledge against experience, rational against emotional, verbal against nonverbal, theory against practice, and so forth.[3] Alas, these are not always valued as equal opposites across the divide. The cognitive, rational side of the divide has often been prioritized as more valuable, while the more embodied elements are deemed inferior.

1. Johnson, *The Body in the Mind*, xxvi–xxvii.
2. Johnson (*The Body in the Mind*, xxviii–xxix) traces Kant's attempt to bridge the epistemological gap between ideas and external reality. Kant's account of imagination is an attempt to understand how sense impressions interact with rational concepts. But Kant ends up reinforcing the mind-body dichotomies because he could not acknowledge the "interactional character of imagination" to help "explain the nature of meaning" (xxix). We will be addressing the imagination's role shortly.
3. Gibbs, *Embodiment*, 4. See also, by the philosopher Esther Meek, *Loving to Know*.

I suspect that part of the reason for this divide and the prioritization of mind over body is related to the worry that if we give attention to the experiential qualities of sensation or emotion, this will lead to or foster a deficit of reason and objective reality. But must these things be mutually exclusive? Does one have to negate the other, or can they work together? In the next section we will begin to explore their integration as we look at more embodied qualities of knowledge, which includes the physical senses. As David Howes states, "A focus on perceptual life is not a matter of losing our minds but of coming to our senses."[4]

Knowing Is Embodied

In the wake of this mind-body divide, and to orient us in our approach to the Gospels, let's examine the premise that our knowing is actually more embodied than we might realize. Recent scholarship across several disciplines demonstrates this corporeal quality of knowledge.

In the 2014 bestseller *The Body Keeps the Score*, Bessel van der Kolk explores the interconnected activities of the brain, mind, and body when one is grappling with past trauma. At the core of van der Kolk's work lies the premise that bodies harbor a kind of knowledge that affects—even reshapes—how people experiencing past trauma both think and live going forward. His findings have led to groundbreaking treatment and recovery for individuals and communities experiencing PTSD from all sorts of past traumas. Van der Kolk's research is significant in demonstrating how integral embodied experience is to our epistemic mental processes.

As we further consider how our bodies are connected to the meaning-making process, think about how our *language* is embodied. In *Metaphors We Live By*, George Lakoff and Mark Johnson highlight how the metaphors we use in our words and thought are dependent on the embodied lives we live. The language we use is grounded in our experience in the physical world. For example, we think and speak in metaphors like GOOD IS UP: "The Market is *up* today." "Are

4. Howes, introduction to *Empire of the Senses*, 7.

you *up* for this?" We might speak of ARGUMENT AS WAR: "I *won* the argument." "She *shot down* all his points." "His critique is *indefensible*." Or we might discuss IDEAS AS FOOD, where a concept might be "hard to *swallow*," or an idea is "*half-baked*," or where we "*digest* the proposal."[5] Metaphors are pervasive in how we think and speak, reminding us of the relevance of embodiment to meaning.

Let's consider another example. Did you know that scientists have discovered that the brain is constantly simulating using mental imagery as we interact with the world? This activity does not consist of purely mental operations; it also involves our bodies. Think about what is involved in sitting down in a chair. Researchers observe how this action is absorbed in the brain's memory through several modalities, including how the chair looks (perception), what it feels like to sit down in it (action), and the memory of the comfort the chair provides (introspection). When knowledge of a chair is later recalled, these memories "are reactivated to simulate how the brain represented perception, action, and introspection associated with it."[6]

As we engage with texts, studies of brain imaging help us understand how we often mentally simulate the imagery narrated. Benjamin Bergen observes how we do this with nonfictional *and* fictional stories or concepts. For example, he observes how each of us will picture in our mind's eye something specific when considering a *flying pig*.[7] Or for any Harry Potter fans out there, what did you imagine *dementors* to look like when you first read about them? How did this change when you viewed the depiction of them in film?

Bergen has observed how when language is phrased in the first or second person, this often prompts readers to simulate themselves into the story as a participant in the narrative action. This has some interesting implications when we consider how Jesus makes the claim, "I am the vine, *you* are the branches." If readers consider themselves to be disciples alongside Jesus's narrative audience, how likely are they to picture their role in the scene as a participant?

5. Lakoff and Johnson, *Metaphors*, 4, 46. Here I follow Lakoff and Johnson's practice of designating metaphors using small caps.
6. Barsalou, "Grounded Cognition," 618. See also Barsalou, "Perceptual Symbol Systems."
7. Bergen, *Louder Than Words*, 17–20.

Now, it must be acknowledged that not everyone visualizes or simulates language and narrative in the same ways. We all come to a text with different experiences, imaginative capacities, preferences, and cultural backgrounds. Some of us might not have any ability to visualize imagery, while others might do this endlessly. The point of this discussion is to draw attention to the ways our embodiment influences and operates within our cognitive rational capacities. Knowledge is more than a disembodied, mental operation.

As we begin to consider the physical senses more specifically, it is worth considering how they figure into our understanding of the world. In some ways all we are doing here is tuning our senses and paying attention to embodied operations that we sometimes enact without even realizing it. In the next section I will trace a history of how the senses have come to be numbered, understood, and valued. I will also discuss the varying roles the senses play in differing cultural contexts, including both the ancient and the modern landscapes.

Coming to Our Senses

As we address the physical senses specifically, let's explore how they fit into this dichotomous trend of dividing mind from body. To do this, we will look at some of our assumptions about the physical senses, the history of how they have been evaluated, and how they operate.

The typical modern Western individual tends to believe that our sense perceptions exist primarily as biologically determined elements of our physical existence. This view presumes that analysis of the physical senses resides primarily in the domain of the sciences. David Howes adds that "science and psychology typically understand perception to be private, internal, ahistorical and apolitical."[8]

Alongside this perspective sits the premise that the sensorium consists of a hierarchy of five senses. From greatest to least, this includes the senses of sight, hearing, smell, taste, and touch. This pentasensory hierarchy is often traced back to Aristotle, who popularized it but did

8. Howes, introduction to *Empire of the Senses*, 3.

not ultimately invent it.[9] This numbering (five) and ranking of the senses (from sight down to touch) has been relatively fixed throughout history due more to custom and tradition than to nature.[10] The five senses have provided a "structuring pattern," whether for scientific, moral, religious, erotic, or other purposes.[11]

As the two highest-ranked senses, sight and hearing are most often linked with philosophy. This has been explained in a number of ways. For example, Philo considered sight to be "queen of the rest" of the senses,[12] while he ranked hearing in second place.[13] Taste, smell, and touch pertained more to basic maintenance of life, associated with cattle and other wild beasts.[14]

Sight has been consistently ranked more highly than hearing. Aristotle may have been the one to initially crown sight as supreme, but its foremost position became more pronounced during the eighteenth century.[15] It was ultimately Enlightenment-influenced developments that preserved the superiority of sight over the other senses, linking it more definitively to rational thought. (One only needs to look at the so-named period, *Enlighten*ment, to discern this visual trend.) In the wake of the scientific revolution, sight functioned as the premier sense in the all-important function of observation. Technology has fostered visual activities at distant and close ranges—think about the invention of the telescope and the microscope.[16] The proliferation of

9. Avrahami (*Senses of Scripture*, 5) identifies Parmenides in the early fifth century BC as the first philosopher to make a distinction between the mind and the senses, while crediting Plato (423–347 BC) with making this distinction popular. Aristotle was Plato's student who ultimately established the senses into a hierarchy.

10. Vinge (*Five Senses*, 9) traces many who have ordered the senses similarly, including Aristotle, Xenophon, Philo, Origen, and Augustine.

11. Vinge, *Five Senses*, 10–11. Alongside Aristotle's more psychological approach, Origen identified the five spiritual senses. Sometimes the senses would be connected to the elements of the universe, the four seasons, the four temperaments, the seven deadly sins, and so forth, leading Vinge to consider these arrangements as more arbitrary than anything.

12. Philo, *On Abraham* 150: *basilida tōn allōn apephēnen.*

13. Philo considers hearing as inferior to sight because it is "sluggish" and "womanish."

14. Philo, *On Abraham* 149. See also Vinge, *Five Senses*, 25.

15. Avrahami (*Senses of Scripture*, 6) names Kant as the one responsible for this elevation, while also calling him a product of his time.

16. Avrahami (*Senses of Scripture*, 7) makes this observation, providing a much fuller account of the history of the senses than is represented here.

printing presses and increased literacy have also contributed to this elevation of the sense of sight.

Even in today's world evidence points to sight as still holding the leading place, associated as it is with paradigms for rational thought and knowledge. For example, we tend to associate gaining knowledge with sight-centric activities like reading books and computer screens, which are often utilized in silent, fragrance-free libraries. Or pay attention to how often you conceive of knowledge using visual language. We often abide by the phrase "Seeing is believing."[17] (Do you *see* what I mean?) Thus, sight is wielded to articulate categories of knowledge, becoming an intuitive part of how we conceive of our rational thought processes.

In recent decades, however, the normativity of this sight-dominant sensorium has been upended as scholars from various disciplines demonstrate how the physical senses are not entirely mediated through biology but are largely experienced and valued according to culture. Anthropologist Paul Stoller was among the pioneers of this insight. After spending many years in Niger with the Songhay community, he concluded that they actually valued taste, smell, and hearing more highly than the sense of sight. Cultural historian Constance Classen has published similar findings that upend the idea that there is a fixed, biologically determined sensorium. For example, the Tzotzil in the Chiapas highlands of Mexico order much of their world according to thermal symbolism: colors, food, and speech are measured according to their levels of heat and cold.[18] The Ongee community in the Andaman Islands orders their world according to odor,[19] while the Desana in the Amazon rainforest order their world according to color.[20]

17. This is actually only half of a fuller quote from seventeenth-century English minister Thomas Fuller. The full quote is "Seeing is believing, but feeling is the truth," which suggests something far different than what the abbreviated phrase conveys.
18. Classen, "McLuhan in the Rainforest," 148–52.
19. Classen, "McLuhan in the Rainforest," 153–57.
20. Classen, "McLuhan in the Rainforest," 157–60. Of course, a color-regulated world is inherently visual. Classen goes on to describe how color symbolism regulates Desana life, ordering their approach to the natural/supernatural, birth/death, health/illness, male/female. A secondary set of sensory symbolic values includes odor, temperature, and flavor (158).

Classen joins a collection of multidisciplinary scholars in the emergence of sensory anthropology, which demonstrates how, as Howes states, "the human sensorium . . . never exists in a natural state. Humans are social beings, and just as human nature itself is a product of culture, so is the human sensorium."[21] Biology is not completely irrelevant, but sensory anthropology demonstrates how even science is culturally mediated. For example, in the field of chemistry, Lissa Roberts describes "the death of the sensuous chemist" as she traces how increasingly complex technologies have come on the scene that require sight for making more "objective" inspections of chemical findings. Consequently, this "new" chemistry has replaced premodern trends that employed more "subjective" sensitive sources of knowledge involving hearing, touch, smell, and even taste.[22] David Howes notes that typically we consider only what DNA *looks* like, and he asks if this "acid with a sugary 'backbone'" might be helpfully examined through the question, "What might it taste like?"[23]

This is a significant observation—that the physical senses are not merely natural phenomena but are culturally determined. Sensory anthropology builds on this by highlighting how sensory hierarchies are preserved because they are connected to dynamics such as social rank.[24] Thus, dominant groups in society typically are connected to the more highly esteemed senses, while subordinate groups are linked to the lesser-valued senses.

To be more specific, certain sense perceptions are often linked to both economic status and gender. So in the ancient world, those of a lower economic status were associated with negative smells. Jerry Toner notes how poorer classes tended to carry the smell of their man-

21. Howes, introduction to *Empire of the Senses*, 3. Sensory anthropology draws on insights from scholars in fields like history, anthropology, sociology, geography, literary studies, psychology, and even neuroscience.
22. Roberts, "Death of the Sensuous Chemist."
23. Howes, introduction to *Empire of the Senses*, 5.
24. One particularly troubling example of this dynamic is how some researchers presented a sensory hierarchy according to their own ethnocentric biases. Classen ("Anthropology of the Senses," 405) presents examples such as Lorenz Oken, who in the early nineteenth century suggested a hierarchy of races based on the hierarchy of senses, leading to the European "eye-man," the Asian "ear-man," the Native American "nose-man," the Australian "tongue-man," and the African "skin-man."

ual labor occupations—such as tanners and fullers. Poor dental hygiene also caused a stench, as did living in crowded quarters.[25] By contrast, upper classes were linked to more pleasant smells. They could afford to exist in spacious living arrangements, and thus they were associated with fragrances produced by their gardens, perfumes, and incense.[26] Physical senses were also ordered by gender. Women typically were associated with the senses hovering around their duties at home, including smell, taste, and touch,[27] while men were connected with the sight and hearing so prevalent in their activities out in the external world.[28] Gender concurrently overlapped with economic status. Thus, while women compared to men would be associated with the "lesser" senses of smell, taste, and touch, an "ideal" woman was also one who modestly remained at home, restricted in terms of what she had access to seeing and hearing. This automatically created a divide between elite, wealthier women, who could afford to live out this "modest" existence, and female servants, who were sent out into the world on their behalf, falling short of this ideal.[29]

Finally, the senses in the ancient world were linked with morality. As Toner states, "The physical and the moral became so intertwined that immorality stank."[30] A common example of this is the morality judgment placed against brothels. Brothels became associated with their stench, and this extended to those who worked there.[31] Manual labor occupations were similarly stereotyped as being of a lesser moral stature because of their close contact with dirt.

These are only a few of the numerous examples we could discuss demonstrating how the physical senses are biological in nature *and* culturally mediated. They are personal *and* corporate. And they are diverse in how they are experienced and valued.

25. Toner, "Sensing the Ancient Past," 6.
26. Classen, Howes, and Synnott, *Aroma*, 33.
27. Classen, "Witch's Senses," 70.
28. Potter ("Social Life of the Senses," 28) notes how the sense of sight was connected with societal power structures. Women were often excluded from certain amphitheater-style entertainment, and when they were included, men were privileged to have the closest seats.
29. Aldrete, "Urban Sensations," 62.
30. Toner, "Sensing the Ancient Past," 7.
31. Toner, "Sensing the Ancient Past," 7.

Our modern context is not much different; the physical senses as we experience them fall into certain hierarchies depending on cultural context. Today we attach the senses to various economic factors, and we also extend morality judgments tied to sense perception. But this is the water in which we swim, so we have to pay attention in order to notice these dynamics; this is the reason for a book like this. As I continue to lay out the backdrop for this study, I invite you into adopting an increased awareness of how the senses function in your own personal and communal settings. Let's continue to reflect on how this will prepare the soil for exploring the sensory aspects of the Gospels.

Bridging the Mind-Body Divide through an Openly Sensory Approach

Recent increased attention to embodiment has begun to blur the mind-body bifurcation in some helpful ways, but the divide persists. (Within this, the sense of sight remains wedded to the rational side of the equation, which in turn holds sight in the premier position over the other senses.) Ultimately, this separation of mind and body is problematic for two interrelated reasons. First, this bifurcation can lead to an undervaluing of embodied knowledge—this has been coined the "brain-on-a-stick" approach.[32]

And this leads to the second problem: anyone and everyone who excludes embodiment from their approach to "knowledge" is embodied. That fact may seem obvious, but we must observe that it is problematic to think that we are understanding something *only* with our minds. This observation pushes back against any suggestion that the most objective thoughts are disembodied. In other words, how do we tacitly yet unthinkingly bring our embodiment to our understanding of a text? Does this at all distort what we *could* be gleaning from it? Do we think that we are approaching the text with our minds alone, when actually we approach it with our minds *and* our bodies,

---

32. So called by J. Smith (*You Are What You Love*, 3), who makes the case that our bodies and nonvisual sense perceptions contribute a certain quality of knowledge to our understanding in general.

without considering whether there is more of our embodiment that we can purposefully include? How might a thoughtfully embodied approach enhance (or change) our understanding of the text, and what can the physical senses contribute to this?

This study is unique in its approach to the text by keeping all the physical senses intact. That is, rather than "bracket out" our sensory knowledge because we think it will tarnish the goal of reading for epistemological, disembodied objectivity, my approach here leans into the reality that all our reading is embodied. This reading of the Gospels, then, will be openly sensory. In our reading we will keep track of our sensory backgrounds and biases, but I hope that we do more. How can we harness our senses toward a more robust understanding of the texts in question?

Hence, as we explore how Jesus repeatedly uses the sense of touch to enact healing (e.g., Matt. 8:3; Mark 1:31; Luke 4:40; John 9:6), we will address ancient receptivity to touch, how Jesus's proximity confers dignity, and how these healings—by their tactile nature—might have transformed the lives of those with whom he interacted. We will consider Jesus's statement "I am the good shepherd" (John 10:11, 14) as he invites sheep to hear his voice calling their name (John 10:3). How does this interact with Jesus's voice calling Lazarus out of the tomb from death to life (John 11:43)? Or what does it mean in the Synoptics when a voice comes from the cloud, saying, "This is my Son. . . . Listen to him!" (Matt. 17:5; Mark 9:7; Luke 9:35)? A sensory reading of the Gospels invites readers to explore ancient contexts in a way that engages the senses, drawing attention to qualities of the abiding life with Christ that are tangible and concrete, dynamic and enduring.

Along the way, I will keep before us the cultural situatedness of the physical senses. We will look at both problematic and helpful ways certain senses may be ranked high—or low. This in turn will open discussion into the personal relativity of the senses. Just as certain cultures use or value some physical senses over others, as individuals we do not all utilize the same number of senses in the same ways. Those who lack the sense of sight likely value other senses—perhaps hearing or smell—more highly than a sighted person might. What can we learn from the significant ways such persons value the senses in ways others might miss? Or think about the variety of comfort levels involved in how we give and receive touch. While some grow up in highly affection-ate families, others are more reserved about sharing affection. Many who survive traumatic, invasive touch experienced through abuse or medical procedures remind us that touch is a highly sensitive, delicate matter, which ultimately highlights its significance and potency.

All of these diversities remind us of the vast, multisensory op-portunities we have to experience the world. We have much to learn from one another. I invite you to adopt a teachable stance in ap-proaching the biblical text as we let this exploration furnish us with an expanded sense of the goodness of God, the ultimate giver of our sensory capacities to experience this sensate life.

The Senses, Imagination, and Memory

Up to this point, we have established that our knowledge is both em-bodied and sensory. We have looked at a history of the senses and their cultural dynamics. And we have also talked about how our sensory lives are diverse. So now, *how* does all of this lead us into a *sensory* reading of the Gospels? The final section of this chapter will complete the scaffolding for our approach. Let's turn now to address the role of imagination, memory, and how our senses help us engage the text.

Imagination: Connecting Sensory Knowledge and Sensory Texts

Imagination is important, but it's often misunderstood. It's the link between the sensate reader and a sensory text, but we often peer at imagination with suspicion, its unruly reputation allied with cre-ativity, fantasy, and subjective thought.[33] We use our imagination to approach *the Word*? Is that permissible? After all, we tend to think of biblical texts as carrying fixed meanings and truth claims. However, has it ever occurred to you that imagination is instrumental to *all* our mental processing and reasoning? Imagination has been associated with Plato's notion of how one formulates an image in the mind's

---

33. This notoriety can, in part, be traced back to Romanticist-era notions of the nineteenth century.

eye. It helps us to conceptualize both fiction and nonfiction as we seek to understand the worlds authors create.

Paul Ricoeur developed a helpful framework for thinking about imagination by presenting it in terms of its reproductive and productive components. Reproductive imagination speaks to the tacit ways we organize our thoughts. As Ricoeur once stated, "There is no such thing as a brute impression, an impression that is direct and unadorned by human structuring."[34] Reproductive imagination speaks to how we structure and understand our mental content, so it is essential to our mental processing. Immanuel Kant described it as a more innate, automatic operation that we engage in without even thinking about it.[35]

By contrast, productive imagination describes the part of our imagination that envisages possibility, encompassing the more creative components of our thought processes. These two elements of imagination may be viewed as existing on a spectrum, and both are critical components of a thriving imagination.[36] In practice, reproductive and productive imaginations function together as a dialogue, so intertwined that they would be difficult, if not impossible, to separate. They work together in conversation, both drawing on and transforming existing categories.[37]

To illustrate this, let's inspect the thought process involved in comprehending a metaphor. When Jesus states, "I am the bread of life" (John 6:35, 48), readers may begin by reflecting on the question "How is Jesus like bread?" The reproductive imagination will furnish one's thoughts with previous conceptual notions of their understanding of

34. Ricoeur, "Lectures on Imagination," quoted in Taylor, "Ricœur's Philosophy of Imagination," 94. Ricoeur cites Austin, *Sense and Sensibilia.* Imagination was quite significant to Ricoeur's thought, yet all we have from him about it are these unpublished lectures, as presented by Taylor, "Ricœur's Philosophy of Imagination."
35. See Johnson, *The Body in the Mind*, 139–72. That chapter, "Toward a Theory of Imagination," highlights the four major stages in the development of Kant's view of imagination, including reproductive imagination, productive imagination, the schematism, and the creative operation of imagination in reflective judgment. For Kant, productive imagination gives us the "structure of objectivity," and reproductive imagination provides "all of the connections by means of which we achieve coherent, unified, and meaningful experience and understanding" (151).
36. See, for example, the insightful employment of the productive-reproductive imagination in Lee, "Imagery."
37. Taylor, "Ricœur's Philosophy of Imagination," 97–98.

"bread." Depending on the readers' level of scriptural awareness, they might think of bread as the manna from heaven in the Exodus narrative, or bread as wisdom, or bread as Torah. Most will also immediately connect Jesus's claim to literal connotations of actual bread.

The productive imagination comes into play as readers begin to survey the possibilities of what Jesus could mean with this claim. Jesus could not possibly be suggesting that he is equivalent to actual flour-yeast-water bread, right? Is there a component of bread to which he is trying to link himself? Readers must imagine the possibilities: What could be the implications of equating Jesus to manna from heaven? To wisdom? To Torah? How do these former conceptions of bread connect with Jesus's claim to be the bread of life? The imagination is critical to comprehending the text in question.

This reproductive/productive imaginative process is rather intuitive; we engage with it fairly automatically. It's probably impossible to pin it down to some regulatable process, since the reproductive and productive elements of our imagination are more like a back-and-forth dialogue. If this feels a little slippery to you, don't be too concerned. I call attention to it to remind us *that* we use our imagination. Rather than fear or shrink back from it, I hope that we can embrace it a bit more.

Imagination, Memory, and the Senses

Let's continue to fill out our understanding of the imaginative process. For this, we return to something that is integral to our reproductive imagination. Remember that reproductive imagination is how we structure our thoughts around comprehension of something like a narrative. When we read a narrative, we draw on our *memories* of what words mean in context. This is where it gets interesting because this is where the senses enter the conversation.

Philosopher Henri Bergson once stated, "There is no perception which is not full of memories. With the immediate and present data of our senses, we mingle a thousand details out of our past experience."[38]

38. Bergson, *Matter and Memory*, 181. Vinge (*Five Senses*, 42) describes Augustine's view of memory and the senses, highlighting its power as being "as wonderful as the most miraculous works in nature."

Similar to how "high-fiving" a palm branch reminds me of high-fiving bystanders on a racecourse, have you ever smelled a fragrance that reminded you of the familiar perfume of a relative? Or have you ever tasted a holiday dessert, triggering a nostalgic memory of past celebrations? Similar to how "the body keeps the score" in terms of trauma, our senses will also lodge memories into our bodies that are often brought to mind when these sensory experiences are repeated.

Now, as we bring our imagination to the sensory aspects of a text, there is obviously a difference between smelling something materially and smelling something imaginatively. But the two are linked, often through memory. When we encounter a sensory element in a text, embodied readers may at times find their own sensory experiences and memories triggered. As we are attentive to these connections, we open ourselves to greater depth of understanding of the layers of meaning presented by the text.

Let's return briefly to how we mentally simulate as we read. Benjamin Bergen has observed how the act of embodied simulation involves our physical senses too. Studies of brain imaging have shown how remembering will "reactivate the same brain circuits [we] originally used to encode the sights, sounds, smells, and feel of the memories in the first place."[39] Thus, when we imagine sound, we do so by using the same brain regions where we hear sound.[40] This is a quality of knowledge that does not come from a book but rather is lodged in someone's sensate past.[41]

How does this work in a narrative? When we read Jesus's claim, "I am the bread of life," those of us who have ever tasted bread will carry an embodied memory of this experience. How might this memory inform our understanding of Jesus's claim? Let's take it further. Jesus also states, "Whoever comes to me will never go hungry, and whoever believes in me will never be thirsty" (John 6:35). Even

39. Bergen, *Louder Than Words*, 42.
40. Bergen, *Louder Than Words*, 35.
41. To give another example, think about how our understanding of a dog is influenced by our embodied experience with one. While one person might have affectionate embodied memories of a loyal, loving, furry companion, another person might have different embodied memories, particularly if in childhood they were bitten by a ferocious dog. Based on these memories, we can understand why one might gravitate toward a neighbor's dog, while another might recoil in fear.

if we haven't tasted bread, humans carry a daily, universal need to be nourished by food in some form. I would venture to guess that we have all experienced hunger. To go from hunger to nourishment is more than mere cognitive knowledge; it's an embodied experience that we know, because we know this nourishment in our guts, literally. How might this quality of sustenance inform our comprehension of the salvific claim that coming to and believing in Jesus means that we will never go hungry or thirsty again?

Reading with Our Senses Intact

The sensory scaffolding is nearly in place. As we prepare to engage the sensory aspects of the Gospel narratives, we hold in the background this reality that we are more than "brains-on-sticks." We have discussed the embodied quality of our language, and we have addressed the idea that our embodied, sensory memories influence how we imagine and comprehend the world around us, including narrative.

One last thing before we move on. I realize that all of this may raise concern for some who fear that this approach is setting up to be more reader-response in character. (A "reader-response" approach is one whereby the meaning of a text can be whatever readers imagine or experience it to mean.) For example, we have acknowledged a wide diversity of sensory backgrounds, values, experiences, and memories. If we all bring such diverse perspectives to the text, this raises the following concern: Are we heading into a land of subjectivity where we can't find any coherent sense of what the narrative is meant to convey?

To clarify, our approach is going to be more historical in character, and it will be largely descriptive. My goal is to paint a more vivid picture of what is going on in the Gospels by highlighting the sensory qualities of the narrative world in its context. Why, then, you might be wondering, is it relevant to discuss our own sensory memories and contexts? Great question! I have two comments in response.

First, think about how we contribute greater embodied understanding to our own world. We understand what bread tastes like by describing it, but even more, by taking a bite of it, chewing, and swallowing. This is a different kind of sensate knowledge. Similarly, can we gain a more fully embodied understanding of a narrative when we ask some sensory questions? These are questions such as, What would it have *smelled* like to be in the room when a woman anointed Jesus with "about a pint"—the equivalent of four or five modern perfume bottles!—of fragrant perfume? You and I can describe strong scents with words all day long. What happens when we consider the effect of strong fragrances in our own worlds? What happens when you light a scented candle or when you take a long whiff of fragrant perfume? Can this get us closer to comprehending what Jesus's disciples witnessed as he let the woman anoint his body? Bringing the senses into our descriptions, I suggest, will help us to comprehend the narratives in more fully embodied ways.

The second comment goes back to this push against our modern tendencies to bracket out—or think that we are bracketing out—our embodiment as we read. To acknowledge that as readers we have sensory embodied knowledge that is not so easily filtered out of our reading means that there will actually always be a small thread of a reader-response approach involved in understanding a text. We can never completely bracket out our embodiment, although perhaps many of us are conditioned to try. But I'm not sure we should. Thus, on the one hand, this book is not about granting license to feel our way to any conclusion we sense. On the other hand, this *is* a book that seeks to harness our sensory lives toward a greater depth of understanding of these Gospel narratives. Through this, I hope that we might be reminded of God's goodness in granting us these fully embodied, sensory lives to know him with all that we are.

With our sensory framework established, we will turn next to address some preliminary considerations about the Gospels themselves. How should we approach these four narratives about Jesus's life, death, and resurrection? What do we make of their similarities, their differences, their overlapping details? What role does history play in these accounts about Jesus? Finally, you might be wondering why we are addressing Matthew, Mark, and Luke together, and John separately. To these matters we now turn.

2

The Focus of Our Sensory Approach

Introducing the Gospels

I love to get lost in a good novel. For me, this typically takes place during a week of summer vacation at my in-laws' condo, where at their community pool there is a free, informal lending library (it's one of those "take a book, leave a book" arrangements). One of my favorite things to do on the first day of our trip is to walk over to the pool to pick out my book(s) for the week. When, in the course of the week, I finish a book, I walk over to the pool and return it. I've left many a novel at that community library, because really, once you've finished the story, when are you ever going to read it again? The mystery is solved, the villain is revealed, the protagonist is vindicated, and you know how it ends, so why read it again?

What Are the Gospels, Exactly?

Gospels are similar to novels in that they are also narratives, but we don't tend to discard the Gospels at the lending library once we've read them. Why not? Well, you might respond, the Gospels are a different *kind* of story. They have historical value; they are presented as being about someone's actual life. Okay, we are getting a little closer: many scholars liken the Gospels to an ancient type of celebrity biography called a *bios*.[1] But still, I would counter, lending libraries carry plenty of nonfictional biographies, discarded upon consumption. What makes the Gospels different from a novel or from a biography?

The missing piece has to do with what the Gospels are and why they were written.[2] They are more than simple biographies about Jesus and were crafted to go beyond informing (and entertaining) us, although they accomplish this as well. What makes the Gospels unique is that these are biographical narratives that are also shaped with theological purpose. The hint is in each being called a "gospel" (*euangelion*), which in Greek means "good news." From creation God has been at work in the world, and God's people Israel had been looking forward to a day when he would come and bring restoration, justice, and healing. And the *good news* is that God has come! Jesus is God's anointed—Messiah—stepping in to fulfill what God began, embodying "the good news of the kingdom" (Matt. 4:23; 9:35; Mark 1:15). And the Gospels tell this story in four-part harmony. Matthew, Mark, Luke, John: here are four overlapping stories about Jesus's birth, ministry, words and deeds, and death and resurrection. Each voice is unique, and yet all four blend together both to disclose and to teach us about who Jesus is and why this matters.

So, the four Gospels are a unique blend of history, narrative, and theology; we can approach them to be informed, and we can read

1. *Bios*, as in the "life" of a person as laid out in ancient biographies. Craig Keener recently coined the term "Christobiography." See Keener, *Christobiography*, where he explores a wide swath of ancient biographies to better understand how the Gospel writers align with the literary practices of their time.

2. To be specific, we are focused here on the four *canonical* Gospels—that is, those gospels that were recognized early as authoritative by consensus among the Christian tradition. This recognition has to do with these Gospels' connection to eyewitness testimony, along with how their content coincides with the theological tradition. There are other "apocryphal Gospels" in existence that are distinct from these four in terms of their form and content. As Campbell and Pennington (*New Testament*, 73) summarize, these Gospels often "vary quite a bit in terms of form, reputation, influence, and value."

them to be instructed. But there is one more insight that will cement for us what the Gospels are, exactly. Significantly, they are written to invite us to be transformed. As part of the canon, the Gospels are meant to be read as Christian Scripture.[3] As Jonathan Pennington and Constantine Campbell state, they are "theological documents with the specific goal of inviting people to become disciples of Jesus."[4] As such, they have formative value. This is why we might be more inclined to keep the Gospels on our bedside tables rather than return them to the lending library.

In the next section we will expand on the categories introduced here. Specifically, as we encounter four Gospels that are both similar and very different from one another, how can we understand their historical value as we focus mostly on narrative details? Moreover, how can we set ourselves up well to understand what the sensory elements contribute to our understanding of and interaction with a very formative set of texts?

Historical Value and Theological Distinctives

If you have ever spent time reading and rereading all four Gospels, you may have raised some of the following questions: Since several of the Gospels are so similar to one another, why are there four of them? Conversely, among the four, why are these stories so different in some key places? If the Gospels present different—even conflicting, at times—details, how can they be historically accurate? Is there one account that "gets it right" in terms of "how it happened" in history?

Notice how these questions are framed around the historical quality of the Gospels. If we approach the Gospels as being biographical, we are immediately confronted with questions about historicity whenever the Gospel stories seem to collide or conflict with one another. This is why it is helpful to understand that these are "theological biographies." In other words, while we can approach the Gospels as being about Jesus in history, we have to understand that the writers also arranged their material in a purposeful, selective manner, keyed

---

3. Campbell and Pennington, *New Testament*, 85–86.
4. Campbell and Pennington, *New Testament*, 72.

specifically to each Gospel's theological purpose. These aren't meant to be read like your standard-issue high school history textbook. Each Gospel emphasizes certain theological themes and insights. And the Gospel writers have shaped their narratives to these ends.

This dynamic has led to debate for many years since it has prompted scholars to suggest that there is a difference between what they would call the "Jesus of history" and the "Christ of faith." That is, many who view the Gospels as being products of the church understand the theological portrait of Jesus to be disconnected from the actual historical Jesus who walked the earth. This line of thought has led some, unfortunately, to discount many (though not all) of the Gospel stories as being fabricated toward theological ends.

A similar dehistoricizing trend materializes in some narrative approaches to the Gospels. Such literary methods address the Gospels for their narrative value alone—inspecting elements such as plot and characterization, for example. In the process they often leave off questions of history altogether. Not all narrative approaches do this, and in fact, such methods have been wonderfully fruitful in uncovering significant emphases presented by the Gospel writers. But it's easy to see how such a focus can lead us to neglect questions about the historical value of the narrated events in the Gospels.

All of this is relevant because we will be looking at all four Gospels and their (at times) differing accounts of a particular scene. And while we will be addressing them primarily as narratives in terms of how the story is being told, this does not mean that they don't have historical value. Theological emphasis and historicity are not *necessarily* mutually exclusive; I think they can be held together. However, there *are* ways history is narrated that are unique to the Gospels as theological biography. The following will highlight some of these dynamics in more detail.

First, the Gospels are not exhaustive in what they share. John, in the very last verse of his Gospel, writes, "Jesus did many other things as well. If every one of them were written down, I suppose that even the whole world would not have room for the books that would be written" (21:25). Have you ever noticed that we get only select stories from Jesus's life? For example, why don't we know anything about his growing-up years? Matthew and Luke tell us about Jesus's birth, and Luke relays one event from his boyhood. But then the story skips all the way to the final few years of Jesus's life—his ministry, death, and resurrection. A huge amount of each Gospel is devoted to the last week of Jesus's life. This observation alone communicates to us that Jesus's death and resurrection are paramount to the writers' telling of the "good news." And this illustrates for us the theological motivations behind how the Gospels are narrated. Because of this, I don't think we need to worry that we don't have all the same details in all four Gospels. It only helps our understanding of each Gospel to consider why the details that we do have were selected.

Second, the Gospels don't necessarily tell the story of Jesus's life in exactly the same sequence, but this does not mean that they don't carry historical value.[5] As we look at all four Gospels together, we can get a general flow of Jesus's life and ministry. But there *are* some differently ordered elements, and again, I don't think we need to be too nervous about this. For example, Luke (4:16–31) reports Jesus reading Scripture in his hometown synagogue of Nazareth as a way to commence his ministry; it's the first thing he is narrated as doing. But in Mark (6:1–6), this memorable scene is placed near the middle of Jesus's ministry. So, when did it *actually* happen? It is nonsensical for it to have happened twice,[6] so it seems that here is an example of how one of the writers rearranged the events to emphasize a certain theme.[7]

In today's smartphone-saturated, media-savvy world, where the details of our lives can be (and are) instantly captured and broadcast to the world, we might unknowingly bring a bit of this backdrop into our interpretation of a Gospel narrative. That is to say, we might

5. The sequencing of the stories may correspond to the historical ordering of the events, but even if the order is not completely the same, Carson, Moo, and Morris (*New Testament*, 53) note that the lack of perfectly aligned chronological sequencing across the Gospels does not reflect "error" so much as it reflects "chronological indifference." Topical arrangement of the material on the part of the evangelists does not rule out historicity.

6. It doesn't make sense for him to return to the same synagogue in Nazareth to read the same passage and deliver the same message.

7. Here's another example: Did Jesus clear the temple at the start of his ministry (John 2:13–25) or near the end (Matt. 21:12–13; Mark 11:15–17; Luke 19:45–46)? Or did he do this twice?

suppose historical accuracy to mean that the Gospels provide us the verbatim, sequential retelling of the life and words of Jesus exactly as they occurred, in real time. Do we read these accounts as if the narrator were there, standing by with scroll and ink, jotting down everything Jesus said, right as he said it? This might be unrealistic because exact chronological order was not widely upheld in other ancient biographies that the Gospels most resemble, and ancient audiences would not expect it.[8] As New Testament scholar Craig Keener writes, "Modern readers sometimes hold the Evangelist[s] to standards that not only deviate from ancient expectations but that modern readers do not follow in ordinary life."[9]

So how *did* the Gospels get to us in the form they are in? By word of mouth, to start. In a culture where oral tradition was more prominent, the kernels of the Gospel stories likely began in oral form, much like how the book of Acts describes the early activities of the church. Disciples of Jesus went out and shared their remembrances about him. They shared his teachings (which they likely knew well if, as we assume, he taught in all kinds of places and settings). And at some point, Jesus's words and works were written down and fashioned into the Gospels as we now have them.

Think about what the Gospels are, then. These are not real-time, unreflective accounts of Jesus's life events strung together in a hurry, like a newscaster rushing up to the scene to provide on-the-hour reporting. Rather, the Gospels are more like an aged wine or a piece of well-marinated meat. The community of Jesus's followers has had time to mull over the implications of the life and words of Jesus from a postresurrection perspective. They have reflected on Jesus in light of what they know of Scripture (which, remember, for them would not include the New Testament). John often writes this retrospect into his Gospel, as he will narrate something to the effect of, "We didn't know it then, but we see it now" (2:22; 20:9). In this way the

8. Keener, *Christobiography*, 138–42.
9. Keener, *Christobiography*, 142. He gives an example illustrating how even as moderns we don't always give or expect chronological, verbatim reports. Consider a parent asking their child upon arriving home from university for the summer what they did this past semester. Nobody gets out their calendar and describes what they did day by day.

Gospels present the fruit of extended reflection on the theological implications of Jesus as the *good news*. And more than ever, the narrators are interested in extending a formational invitation for readers to respond in faith (e.g., John 20:31).

Our Approach to the Four Gospels

The Synoptics and John

With some basic background on *what* the Gospels are and their purpose, let's turn to this sensory study and address how we will approach them. If you have read all four Gospels, you may notice that Matthew, Mark, and Luke are very similar to one another; for this reason we call these the *Synoptic* Gospels.[10] The Synoptics share a high degree of verbal similarity.[11] Based on this, most believe that there is a literary relationship among them.[12] Today it is widely believed that Mark was written first (as the shortest account), while Matthew's and Luke's Gospels are variations (and expansions) of Mark's material based on their own theological aims. There is more we could say about this, but this is simply to explain why I will address the Synoptic Gospels as a unit in our sensory study. There are several places where two or more of the Synoptics present a certain sensory scene, and at times they may even vary their sensory details. We won't address who might have relied on whose account or why one writer includes certain details compared to another. I will simply be calling attention to relevant sensory similarities and differences. I will also point out any pertinent sensory scenes that might not be represented by all three.

John's Gospel is a different animal. There is agreement and similarity regarding the "basics" of Jesus's life and ministry—he was

---

10. "Synoptic" comes from the Greek word *synopsis*, which in essence means "seen together."

11. Of the 661 verses in Mark, 500 recur in Matthew in parallel form, and 350 recur in Luke. There are another 235 verses common to Matthew and Luke that are not found in Mark.

12. To those who might push against this conclusion, supposing that each writer happened to write down a similar version of the same oral account, consider that even if they are hearing the same teaching, they are writing in one language (Greek) something they might have heard originally in another (Aramaic).

baptized, he had disciples, he performed miracles, he died on a cross and was resurrected—but John tells it quite differently. This is one reason why it is believed that John's Gospel was compiled later and independently from the Synoptics.[13] Because of this difference we will address the sensory elements in John mostly separate from the Synoptics. In John, many of the sensory details are wrapped up into Jesus's words and statements about himself, and these will sometimes converge with his works. You might notice that these insights revolve around several of the seven "I am" sayings and their related signs and events, although other sensory passages will also figure into the discussion.

Which Readers Are We Talking About?

In chapter 1 we established that our focus is on the sensory elements present in the Gospel narratives. Hence, we are concerned about *how* the stories are told. At the same time, the Gospel stories were composed in a first-century context, and the narrated events are situated in this same ancient, historical setting. Against this backdrop there are certain values placed on the sensory elements. Therefore, our first look at the text will be at how the senses would have been operating in these events within the world of the narrative. How would the characters experience them? From here we will inspect how the earliest readers might have understood these dynamics.

Now, when we talk about how "readers" engage a text, the truth is there are many types of readers involved. Narrative-critical approaches to texts will identify, for example, the "implied reader," which references the type of reader the story is narrated for. This is similar (though not identical) to the category of "ideal" reader. Basically, the "implied" or "ideal" reader is aligned with who the author wants to reach. This is who the author hopes will follow the contours of his or her purposes. To use the example of John's Gospel, the implied or ideal reader is identified as someone for whom the stated purpose of the Gospel comes to fruition: belief (20:30–31).

---

13. Recent scholarly conversations have explored the question of whether John knew or relied on Mark, but John is really quite different from the Synoptics.

Now—stay with me here—the "ideal" or "implied" reader typically is distinguished from the "real" reader. The "real" reader, as you might guess, is the actual flesh-and-blood reader of the text: you and me and any reader of the Gospels across the centuries, including the earliest, original readers. The "real" reader might have any number of responses to the Gospel narrative: he or she may align with the "ideal reader" category by responding in belief, or maybe not.

There is another way to classify these "real" readers, which is the distinction between ancient and modern readers. As we consider the sensory qualities of the text alongside the sensory experiences that *any* reader might bring *to* the text, an ancient and a modern reader may understand the value and impact of the sensory elements quite differently. This study's approach to the narrative will first focus on how *ancient* readers might have understood the sensory elements of the narratives. Within this it must be pointed out that just as the "modern reader" is not a monolithic construct (we are all different when approaching the text), neither are ancient readers: they would not have read the text in the same way! A Palestinian Jewish reader, for example, might have interacted with the text differently than an Ephesian gentile reader. I will do my best to outline these diversities in relevant places. But ultimately, what you will see is an unfolding of the ancient sensory contexts for the real, ancient readers.

This approach is not much different than when we read the text to understand its original historical context. Typical historical-critical methods of studying the Bible try to understand what life was like in the ancient world in order to get a fuller picture of the implications of Jesus's words. For example, it's helpful to know that Roman crucifixion was a very shameful form of execution in its day. This helps us understand the magnitude of the humiliation that Jesus was subject to as he suffered death on the cross. With a sensory approach we are trying to do a similar thing but with a focus on the physical senses. For example, the fragrance of perfume is quite potent. Have you ever been subject to someone's strong perfume when they walked into a room? Have you ever wondered how long Jesus smelled like fragrant perfume after he was anointed by the woman during a meal? In a world where bathing was not likely a daily occurrence, perhaps Jesus and his disciples were reminded of her gesture for days (because the scent literally lingered on his skin!). As we consider and imagine the sensory dimensions of the narrative scene, how do the senses add rich and robust colors and flavors to the text?

Narrative is such a compelling invitation to imagine ourselves into the story. In engaging the Gospel narratives, all readers, ancient and modern, are invited to connect empathically with the characters. The trick for us will be to navigate the imaginative gulf between ancient and modern readers.[14] What do I mean by this? Well, when I say "fragrance," you might imagine something like your dad's cologne at a family birthday party. This may differ from what an ancient reader may think of. Maybe they hear "fragrance" and think of incense burning in the streets during a Roman military triumphal procession. As modern readers, then, we must maintain awareness that this difference exists and work to appreciate the effect that the sensory imagery may have had on the ancient reader.

Putting this all together, then, as we read about Jesus engaging with a hungry crowd, feeding them bread, and then telling them, "I am the bread of life," we will have a chance to consider how the crowd's hunger and thirst prompt memories of hunger and thirst in ancient readers. Part of how we align empathetically with these characters is through our own understanding of hunger and thirst. On one level, this imaginative exercise can provide us with greater understanding about the ancient context in all its sensory richness. We can walk away having mentally considered the implications of symbolic "hunger and thirst" for God.

But this takes us only so far. What happens when we consider our own embodied experiences of hunger and thirst and apply them to symbolic readings of hunger and thirst for God? With the formational aim of the Gospels in view (which we opened this chapter with), how does it transform our understanding of hunger for God as we infuse our own embodied experience with hunger to this category of need? This is the embodied fullness of the sensory approach that I invite you to engage with.

14. I have written in more detail about this in Hanger, *Sensing Salvation*, 32.

Sensory Invitations and Sensing the Holy Spirit

And really, this is what the Gospels do: they invite us to engage. They do more than entertain; they do more than inform us about what Jesus said and did. And they do more than teach us why he came and why we should care. The invitation of the Gospels is for us to ponder, to make connections, and to respond. The Gospels invite us to engage with Jesus himself.

As the Gospel writers present, Jesus is the anointed one, sent from God to inaugurate the kingdom. John says that Jesus is "the Word," who was with God in the beginning (a nod to the creation account in Gen. 1:1) and is himself God. Do we believe that this is true? It's really easy in our day to think of "truth" as a disembodied idea that must be abstract and repeatable to be considered valid and real. But Jesus comes as an embodied person, in the flesh, and he makes this bold claim, saying, "I am the truth" (John 14:6). This is a very personal, particular kind of truth.[15]

Jesus then invites all kinds of people to believe and entrust themselves to him through his word and his works. For example, in John, "Come and see" is Jesus's call into faith and discipleship (1:39), while in Matthew there is Jesus's repeated invitation, "Follow me" (4:19; 8:18–22; 9:9). Notice how his language invites us to engage our whole selves. Both invitations imply embodied effort to stay near Jesus. And, while this is an invitation extended to characters within the narrative, we can also think of this invitation as being for us too.

This is because all readers are invited to adopt the "ideal reader" category of the Gospels, which is to respond in faith to the invitation to engage with the one who initiates life and restores our broken, fallen world. Thus, the impetus for a sensory study like this is to gain a fuller, embodied understanding of this invitation to abide with Christ. Such a relationship is, by design, very good. But do we *know* this beyond some words we give mental assent to? Can we sense it?

15. Watkin (*Biblical Critical Theory*, 359) states, "For those who labor under the Enlightenment prejudice that ultimate reality must be . . . pure, abstract and universal, the notion that God could have a body is indeed a scandal." For Watkin's helpful discussion of the historical, time-bound, embodied, personal particularity of the incarnation, see 341–70.

Does it seem as true to you as the taste of bread, the sight of a colorful flower, or the sound of waves crashing on the shore? How can we know God and his goodness more with every part of ourselves?

One of the things we haven't discussed is the role of the Holy Spirit. Within the Gospels themselves, the Holy Spirit is narrated as descending to abide with Jesus (Matt. 3:16; Mark 1:10; Luke 3:22; John 1:32). The Spirit abides with Jesus throughout his life and ministry, and before Jesus departs he introduces the Spirit's abiding presence to his disciples. If you, reader, call yourself a follower of Jesus, then he is present for you too. The Spirit, for Jesus's disciples, is an advocate (John 14:16), an ever-present helper providing direction and wisdom (14:26; 16:13). This is a presence likened to the most satisfying, thirst-quenching, living water (John 4:13–14; 7:37–39). And it is by this Spirit that readers of the Gospels are able to fully comprehend the implications of the texts we will explore.

Therefore, as we move into the actual sensory study (finally, it's time!), I encourage you to invite the Spirit to illuminate your senses to the text in ways you may not have considered. I encourage you to adopt an awareness of your own sensory world, to ask how God has moved and is moving through the sights, sounds, smells, tastes, and touches of your life. And I invite you to just remain open. Be open to what he is doing all around you and to what he is inviting you into as you engage with these texts with your whole self.

3

Tasting the Good Life

Jesus, Bread for the Hungry

Have you ever been hungry? Like really and truly hungry? I don't presume to speak for everyone in the modern West, but I would venture to guess that many of us are unfamiliar with real hunger. Every so often I will skip (or skimp on) a meal, and in the aftermath I will make the offhand comment to anyone within earshot, "I am staaaaarving!" But really, I have never known the kind of hunger born from an actual sustained lack of resource.

Perhaps the closest some of us ever get to hunger is when attempting to engage in a fast. In my own rather limited experience, my fasting will quickly produce hunger pangs that later will lead to physical weakness. During one particular experience, these physical effects of hunger permeated into my emotional state also. That is, I *felt* the vulnerability of my hunger. There was physical consequence due to a lack of calories, but this also dismantled my holistic sense of internal resource. The typical resolve that I habitually muster up to lead myself through a given day and its responsibilities evaporated. In its place was a sense of vulnerability: I felt physically, mentally, spiritually, and emotionally defenseless. Any demands, pressures, or confrontations headed my way, whether verbally or otherwise—I could tell they would hurt. The best way to describe this hunger is that its physical consequences infiltrated to deeper layers of my soul's sense of satiation. My usual sense of autonomy and self-sufficiency thinned to the point where all I knew was my dependence. I knew in my body that I was in need—not just for physical calories but also for other kinds of sustenance. My hunger gave me an invitation to figure out where to seek nourishment.

In what ways does our physical hunger correlate to other kinds of hunger? If hunger signals that our bodies have a need, that we are lacking in nutrients, can it also help us comprehend the significance of Jesus's claim that he is the bread of life (John 6)? Is this a bread for a different kind of hunger? Or to take another angle, what are the implications of the kingdom of God being likened to a great banquet, a celebratory communal sharing of food and drink (Luke 14)? How might our experiences of physical hunger and nourishment prepare us to understand what is involved in the imagery suggesting that life in the kingdom of God is like a huge communal feast, or that Jesus *is* bread?

Exploring Taste

Before we survey the Gospel passages, let's consider taste for a minute. We probably do not give it much thought beyond the pleasures it brings to our eating-and-drinking routines. But taste is a category of knowledge unlike any other. I could spend a thousand words describing to you what bread tastes like, but you will never really *know* its taste until you sink your teeth into that soft doughy substance encased in fresh chewy crust. In this way taste is highly informative and complex. Someone once described it as a "scout" for the foods we eat.[1] Taste is also rarely neutral—one can consume any number of edible and potable items that will range from delightful to disgusting, and this varies from person to person and culture to culture.

Recently we observed how COVID-19 brought taste to the forefront of the conversation for those who noticed *missing* taste as a symptom of the virus. Of course, we know we can survive without

1. Korsmeyer, "Perspectives on Taste," 1.

taste, even though its absence demotes eating and drinking to rote and obligatory actions. But, subsuming all ingestion-related operations under the sense of taste, taste is a vital physical sense, since we *cannot* live without the nutritive sustenance that eating and drinking provide.

Taste is also extremely intimate. We can use our eyes to inspect a lot about the world at both distant and close ranges. We can view bread through a telescope or under a microscope; but it never gets as close as when we ingest it into our bodies. I wonder if this is why Jesus's hearers are so shocked by his statement "My flesh is real food and my blood is real drink" and by his invitation to eat and drink them (John 6:53–56). They would not have to consciously think about how taste is both intimate and nonneutral; they subliminally know in their bodies that eating flesh and drinking blood connoted direct engagement—ingestion—of substances foreign to their religious and cultural sensibilities, and this would trigger a sense of disgust. Their bodies would struggle to accept what Jesus was inviting them to do.

In the rest of this chapter we will wander through select texts in the Gospels that draw on taste, including eating and drinking. As we survey these scenes, I invite you to use your imagination. Place yourself there. Think about your own embodied experiences of hunger and thirst and about how you sit down to a meal to find nourishment. What is it like to be hungry and to have this hunger satiated, or to be thirsty and to have this thirst quenched? What are some implications for being invited to a celebratory meal, for relating to Jesus as the host of a banquet, whether he is giving out bread or embodying the very bread he offers?

Tasting, Eating, and Drinking in the Synoptics

Throughout the Synoptics, Jesus sits down to a lot of meals with people. Communal meals and dinner parties in the ancient world were important social rituals. Compared to many of our on-the-go meal routines, and in the absence of today's drive-through, "working lunch," mobile-order technologies, the ancient world held space for extended and leisurely gatherings over food and drink.

In the ancient context, meals and banquet settings were more than merely a chance to share good eats. This was an important context for fellowship and cultivating friendship over a meal. Such occasions were also highly stratified: it mattered who was invited, how the seating was arranged, and what was discussed. Banquets were always an opportunity for the attainment of honor and the strengthening of a family's reputation through the articulation of hospitality, generosity, and measured reciprocity.[2] As you might imagine, Jesus interrupted the status quo with his own banqueting practices and theories. He often utilized these meals to teach about the kingdom of God and God's heart toward his people.

How Not to Dine and the Kingdom Feast

For example, at a prominent Pharisee's house one Sabbath, Jesus begins to instruct the guests after he watches them select the places of honor at the table (Luke 14:1–24). This prompts a parable about a wedding feast, where after the guests selected for themselves the seats of honor, someone of higher status arrived. The host had to disrupt and downgrade the self-seated guests to a lesser spot to accommodate the honored latecomer. In light of this humiliation, Jesus encourages listeners to approach the table with a humble posture. Take the *lowest* seat at the party, Jesus says—better to be honored with an upgrade.

But Jesus isn't done disrupting the balance of mutual exchange that banqueting practices fostered. Jesus tells the host that instead of inviting those who can reciprocate, invite those who *can't* repay you. Then you will find your reward at the resurrection of the righteous (Luke 14:13–14). Jesus basically upends their expectations about ideal dining practices; he challenges them to think outside their stratified norms of reciprocity.

In response to this instruction, a fellow dining companion exclaims, "Blessed is the one who will eat at the feast in the kingdom of God!" (Luke 14:15). Jesus affirms this friend's joy and launches into a parable describing this grand eschatological banquet. It is notable that when Matthew's Jesus tells this parable, he inserts messianic

2. Chen, *Luke*, 204–5.

tones by specifying it as a wedding banquet in honor of the host's
son.[3] One of the texts potentially evoked by Jesus's anticipation of
this banquet is Isaiah 25:6–8, which presents a similar picture of the
eschatological age as a joyful, extravagant meal in the presence of
God. Let this passage settle into your imagination as a backdrop for
Jesus's parable:

> On this mountain the LORD Almighty will prepare
>   a feast of rich food for all peoples,
> a banquet of aged wine—
>   the best of meats and the finest of wines.
> On this mountain he will destroy
>   the shroud that enfolds all peoples,
> the sheet that covers all nations;
>   he will swallow up death forever.
> The Sovereign LORD will wipe away the tears
>   from all faces;
> he will remove his people's disgrace
>   from all the earth.
>   The LORD has spoken.

The kingdom, as we see, is portrayed as a splendid, joyous feast.
As we turn now to Jesus's presentation of the banquet scene, the
first thing to notice is the generosity of the host. The host is not
skimping on resources and accommodations, since he is hoping to
fill up his house with guests (Luke 14:23). "The more the merrier,"
as the saying goes. When the deluxe banquet itself is ready, the host
is eager to get the party started, so he sends out his servants to call
everyone on the guest list to come. Sadly, many change their RSVP
to no, offering a number of excuses. This angers the host, but notice
that he is not going to force these invitees to come.[4] In this uptick

---

3. Matthew's Jesus shares similar details although in a slightly different setting
during Passion week. In this telling, the banquet is aimed toward a broader view of
salvation history, and the focus is more on Jewish and gentile rejection and acceptance of the invitations to the party. For a fascinating comparison of the Matthean
and Lukan scenes, see Story, "All Is Now Ready."
4. In Matthew's account the host is angry because the invited guests mistreat
and kill his servants.

of declines, he opens the door wide to anyone the servants can find. Note the urgency of the invitation: "Go out quickly into the streets and alleys of the town and bring in the poor, the crippled, the blind and the lame" (14:21). According to Matthew, Jesus says that the host sent out servants who "gathered all the people they could find, the bad as well as the good" (Matt. 22:10).

In ancient Middle Eastern cultures, where meals were a place to display and foster stratified, measured hospitality, where only those who could reciprocate were invited, and where even one's assigned seat indicated their value on the societal scales, God's kingdom banquet throws open the door for anyone and everyone. All are invited, especially those who cannot reciprocate. Hospitality is extravagant and generous, not calculated. Community is inclusive and welcoming, not selective. And if Isaiah has anything to say about it, the shared meal will be delicious; with an abundance of fine wine and top-grade meats, no one is going hungry, and all will recline together—with shame removed and joy abounding.

Thus, Jesus presents this parable of the kingdom as a place of welcome. In the next banquet scene, we are going to see Jesus living this out in real time. He is not talking about a future day but demonstrating by his actions that the kingdom is already here. This disrupts expectations and proper decorum, as we see in how his actions are received by some. God's heart envisions a feast that is different than what many expect. For those who are receptive to Jesus, this is a *better* kind of different, while those who think it's a *worse* kind of different might be the ones who decline the invitation in the end.

Jesus and His Dining Companions

This next meal begins with the calling of Matthew—or Levi, as he is called by Mark and Luke.[5] Jesus invites Levi into discipleship with the summons, "Follow me,"[6] and Levi responds favorably. Leaving

5. Matt. 9:9–13; Mark 2:13–17; Luke 5:27–32.
6. This thematic invitation into discipleship shows up in all four Gospels, including Matt. 4:19–20; 8:22; 10:38; 16:24; 19:21; Mark 1:16–18; 8:34; 10:21; Luke 9:23; 18:22; John 1:43; 10:27; 12:26; 21:19.

behind his post at the toll booth, Levi is doing more than taking a temporary leave of absence; he is permanently vacating his position. As a tax collector, Levi is likely giving up a lucrative job. Tax collectors were employed by Rome to collect all kinds of fees, including imports, exports, road tolls, and income and property taxes.[7] In doing so, they were permitted to collect beyond the amount that was actually owed; and they did this. For most Jewish communities, there was no love lost for these fellow Jews employed by their foreign oppressor as they extracted exorbitant, oppressive fees. As such, tax collectors were considered traitorous and were an understandably despised bunch. And, since tax collectors were constantly interacting with Romans, they were considered ceremonially unclean by the most pious Jews concerned with ritual purity.

So when we read that Levi—probably out of gratitude—throws a banquet for Jesus (Luke 5:29), and Jesus *attends*, well, this is going to be a bit too much for the religious leaders to stay quiet about. Note that the guest list at *this* dinner party includes all of Levi's friends, including a "large crowd" of other tax collectors (and "sinners").[8] This prompts the Pharisees' question, "Why does your teacher eat with *them*?"

Now, in ancient dining practice people typically ate with only those of a similar stripe and status.[9] A Pharisee concerned with remaining ceremonially clean avoided eating in settings where they risked defilement. This means that it is improbable they would ever set foot in the house of a tax collector or sinner. And they would likely expect Jesus and his disciples to follow suit.

Well, Jesus is going to respond very purposefully to their critique. He is not merely defending his actions; his words are going to invite

---

7. Stein (*Mark*, 126) distinguishes between a tax and a toll collector, noting that *tax* collectors handled income and property tax, while *toll* collectors monitored customs and road tolls. Levi was more likely a toll collector stationed on the Via Maris trade route, which ran through Capernaum between Damascus and Caesarea.

8. Matt. 9:10, Mark 2:15, and some manuscripts of Luke 5:29 refer to both tax collectors and sinners. This combination of terms is seen elsewhere (e.g., Luke 15:1). Tax collectors are also collocated with other dishonorable actions and people groups. They are associated with extortion (Luke 3:12–13); robbers, evildoers, and adulterers (Luke 18:11); prostitutes (Matt. 21:32); and pagans (Matt. 18:17).

9. Strauss, *Mark*, 133.

these spiritual leaders to reflect on how their own dining practices reflect (or do not reflect) God's heart. Jesus quotes a known proverb about how it's the sick who need a doctor, not the healthy. And then he says, "But go and learn what this means: 'I desire mercy, not sacrifice'" (Matt. 9:13a). He follows this up with a statement about why he has *not* come, which reverberates with messianic and christological purpose when you consider its opposite: "I have *not* come to call the righteous, but [I *have* come to call] sinners" (9:13b).[10]

Matthew's Jesus hints at the ignorance of the religious leaders when he commands them to "go and learn." He wants them to consider the prophetic call to mercy rather than sacrifice (Hosea 6:6). Jesus is saying to them, in essence, *Guys, let's not be overly concerned about ritual impurity to the exclusion of mercy.* There is more at stake here. Jesus has welcomed sinners, the sick who need a physician; he is unconcerned about the walls erected by religious performance.

So what we have seen to this point is the radical nature of Jesus's association with tax collectors and sinners. The surprise and critique generated by Jesus's actions must be due to the societal separation that had governed these groups of people over time. If the spiritual leaders of Jesus's day were not in the habit of associating with tax collectors and sinners, then Jesus doing so in the name of God introduces a corrective into the landscape. God desires to extend mercy to sinners, and Jesus embodies his Father's heart. This prompts a tax collector to leave his profession to join with Jesus, and he throws a party in celebration and gratitude. In many ways this meal represents the salvific union of a sinner forgiven by God through Christ.

To grasp the fuller implications of this, I invite you to imagine yourself in Levi's home, reclining at the table. When Jesus arrives, he is not merely dropping in for a quick visit as a polite, obligatory show of acceptance of Levi's hospitality. No, Jesus is fully present. He is unconcerned about appearances. As Jesus settles in to recline at the table with a roomful of tax collectors and sinners, remember that he is a Jewish rabbi eating with a people accustomed to being

10. Stein (*Mark*, 131) points out that this does not imply that there are righteous people who don't need Jesus, but instead perhaps Jesus means that he has not come for "those who think themselves righteous."

on the receiving end of the narrowed eyes of religion. They exist on the outside of what is considered pious. They are accustomed to a measure of separation from the revered spiritual leadership. Jesus, however, has drawn close to them. Think about what it would mean to someone like Levi to break bread with Jesus. There is something in the embodied act of sharing a meal that sows unity and friendship into an interaction. Just as two enemies shaking hands both symbolizes and expresses reconciliation, this meal presents a "visual declaration of the offer of forgiveness."[11] In this way Jesus's very presence may carry a message, extending forgiveness to all sinners in Jesus's orbit.[12]

This banquet represents the heart of Jesus for all who need forgiveness. As we accept his invitation to follow him, he invites us to the party. *Let's eat. You can sit by me.* This is a good, abundant meal with the joy and laughter shared by friends. As we turn to our final Synoptic example, let's look at how Jesus continues to extend an invitation into relationship to all through shared meals.

Jesus Feeds the Multitudes

The Gospels report Jesus feeding a multitude of people on at least two different occasions, but it might seem like more, since *all four* Gospels report about the feeding of the "five thousand men" (which would not account for the women and children also present—Jesus fed far more!).[13] The second meal counts four thousand men, and this one is reported only by Matthew and Mark.[14]

In the first feeding, all three Synoptics mention several similar details. Just prior to this feeding Jesus has learned that his cousin John has been beheaded. Matthew notes how this prompts Jesus to withdraw to a solitary place (Matt. 14:13), presumably to get his heart around this development, to mourn this loss. Mark and Luke also mention Jesus withdrawing with his disciples to a solitary place to rest, although this seems related to the disciples returning from ministry activities with which they had been engaged (Mark 6:31;

11. Stein, *Mark*, 128.
12. Stein, *Mark*, 128.
13. Matt. 14:13–21; Mark 6:30–44; Luke 9:10b–17.
14. Matt. 15:32–39; Mark 8:1–10.

Luke 9:10). The bottom line is that Jesus and his friends need some alone time, so they pull away.

We don't know how much solitude they enjoy before the crowds are out searching (and finding) Jesus and his disciples. Mark describes the crowd as being like sheep without a shepherd (Mark 6:34). Jesus is overcome by compassion for them, and he promptly engages with them both to teach and to heal their sick. As the afternoon wears on and evening approaches, the disciples must be sensing the need to wrap things up for the night. My guess is that the disciples got a taste of rest and solitude earlier, and they were eager to get back to it. As they anticipated the physical hunger of the crowd, the disciples had perhaps determined that they had poured out all the resource they had to offer for the day. It was time for Jesus to "call it," and time for the crowd to step up and take care of their own needs: "Send the people away so they can go buy themselves something to eat" (Matt. 14:15; Mark 6:36; Luke 9:12). *We've done enough, Jesus.*

In true shepherd form, Jesus is concerned for his hungry sheep. He notably involves his disciples in the solution—*Hey, friends, you give them something to eat.* As the disciples cobble together the mere bits of food they can find, are they speculating with pessimism, *Jesus, what on earth can be done? This need is beyond us.* Jesus simply takes the five loaves and two fish, looks up to heaven, gives thanks, breaks the bread, and gives it out to his disciples to distribute to the people. All four Gospels note how the people ate until they were "satisfied" (John says that they ate "as much as they wanted"). Amazing! This was no mere pastry snack during happy hour to tide the crowd over until they could get home to the real meal. This was *the* meal. And as is noted in four-part harmony, there were leftovers. I imagine Jesus with a twinkle in his eye—*See what can be done with a few loaves, guys?*—watching each of the twelve disciples pick up a basket of leftover bread as they packed it in for the night.

The feeding of the four thousand is similar in character. Most scholars consider this scene significant for its location in gentile territory; Jesus has come to satisfy the hunger of gentiles too. As Jesus heals their sick, the people stay on. After three days together, the crowd is hungry. Being in a remote location, Jesus's compassion prompts concern that they might "collapse on the way" home to get food (Matt. 15:32). So again, he multiplies the bread and fish, and again, the crowd eats till they are satisfied. And, you guessed it, there are leftovers.

These feeding scenes are widely interpreted as having both past and future resonance. For scripturally attuned readers, this feeding clearly hearkens back to the exodus generation. After Moses led Israel miraculously out of Egypt, the people soon grew hungry as they wandered through the desert. Before too long Israel went from hungry to *hangry*, and they grumbled against Moses, Aaron, and the Lord (Exod. 16). Day after day, God rained down bread—called manna—from heaven, and throughout their wanderings the people gathered as much as they needed. Jesus's miraculous feedings also resonate with prophetic acts like that of Elisha, who multiplied twenty loaves of barley bread to feed a hundred men, with bread left over (2 Kings 4:42–44).[15] Thus, as God miraculously nourishes his people through Moses and Elisha, we see him do the same through Jesus. In terms of its future resonance, Jesus's feeding of the multitudes is widely considered a preview of this messianic banquet that we explored earlier. As Mark Strauss notes, this is a scene depicting eschatological salvation, marked by "peace, prosperity, and abundance (Isa. 25:6; 35:1–10; 51:3; 55:1–2; 60:5–6)."[16]

Finally, Gospel readers cannot but wonder at the formulaic words used, presented nearly identically across the Synoptics, as Jesus initiates the meal: "Taking the five loaves and the two fish and looking up to heaven, he gave thanks and broke the loaves. Then he gave them to his disciples to distribute to the people" (Mark 6:41; cf. Matt. 14:19; Luke 9:16).[17] This is Last Supper language, and Luke uses similar words at the Emmaus meal, when the risen Christ appears to the

15. There are also connections to Elijah's ministry, such as when Obadiah supplied a hundred prophets with food and water in two caves, "fifty in each" (1 Kings 18:13), which Edwards (*Luke*, 266), recognizes as connected to Luke's Jesus telling the disciples to have the people sit in groups of fifty each (Luke 9:14).

16. Strauss, *Mark*, 277.

17. Edwards (*Luke*, 266) notes that this "preserves the memory of the church with greater unanimity than perhaps any other single text in the four Gospels." This perhaps is a result of the church seeing a parallel here between the feeding and the Last Supper.

disciples (Luke 24:30). In each scene, the breaking and giving of bread to the disciples "is a revelatory symbol of Jesus's self-giving for the church in his passion and resurrection, through which the disciples recognize him (24:31) as the fulfillment of Scripture (24:32)."[18]

In these Synoptics feeding scenes the crowds had been hungry, but this did not start out as physical hunger. It was a hunger—a yearning—to be near Jesus, to hear what he was going to say. It was a hunger for him to touch their sick and heal them, to bring them hope. This was perhaps a hunger straining toward the question, "Is he *the one* we are waiting for?"[19] The crowds were so hungry for Jesus that they couldn't even tear themselves away to get something to eat. Jesus fills their hunger in more ways than one, and the wilderness banquet provides the crowd with an embodied experience of having their physical hunger satiated. I wonder how this paired with the other yearnings that held them captive to Jesus's presence.

The meals narrated in the Synoptics surely impress on us the radical generosity of God. This is embodied in Jesus's welcome of all kinds of people, in his compassionate provision of abundant food, and in the picture of joy, forgiveness, and friendship offered to those who are hungry enough to accept the banquet invitation. Turning now to the Gospel of John, let's continue to look at the nature of hunger and how John suggests that our hunger and thirst are satisfied by Jesus.

Tasting, Eating, and Drinking in John

The Fourth Gospel is well known for its rich imagery, so it should not be a surprise that there is quite a bit of eating and drinking throughout. In addition to what we will discuss below,[20] there are meals such as the one celebrating the raising of Lazarus (John 12:1–8) and the Last Supper (13:1–30). Jesus drinks wine from the sponge on

---

18. Edwards, *Luke*, 267.

19. We will get to John's account in the next section, but John 6:14 reports that they surmise this was "the Prophet" who is to come into the world.

20. We won't be able to cover every scene involving food, drink, or a meal, and in fact others have done this in other places. See, for example, Webster, *Ingesting Jesus*.

the hyssop at his death (19:28–30), and he also cooks a breakfast of bread and fish for his disciples (21:1–14). In the rest of this chapter we will simply look at two scenes, one involving drink and the other involving food. In the Synoptics passages we focused on meals in communal settings. Here we will zero in on the act of eating and drinking and how taste operates.

Tasting the Kingdom Life

The wedding in Cana is one of the few scenes in John in which the word "taste" appears. Jesus changing water into wine is the first sign that he enacts in the Gospel of John (John 2:1–11). The following will dance over the relevant details that correspond to themes we have already encountered.

First, this sign occurs at a wedding banquet, which is significant on many levels. For one thing, we get to see Jesus partaking with this community in an extended time of celebration and feasting, a further testament to the joy inherent in God's kingdom vision. But the symbolism of this as a *wedding* feast is really turned up when Jesus saves the host family from public shame after they run out of wine early in the celebration. Jesus responds in this distressing moment by instructing the servants to fill six stone jars with water that typically are used for ceremonial washing. John narrates that when the master of the banquet *tastes* the wine that moments before was just water, he does not know where it has come from (2:9). But the servants know it has come from Jesus. The steward proceeds to honor the bridegroom for saving the choice wine—the best—for now.

The kingdom connotations are hard to miss here. Jesus performs the function of the bridegroom by providing an abundant amount of the *best* wine.[21] Recall the eschatological feast pictured in Isaiah 25:6–8, where God serves a banquet including the finest of aged wine. Amos 9:13–14 also mentions the new wine that will drip from the mountains and flow from all the hills, as God promises to bring Israel back from exile. In this moment we get a picture of Jesus's

---

21. The six stone jars each held 20–30 gallons. If each jar is filled to the brim, we are looking at 120–80 gallons of wine.

messianic vocation, now underway with this first sign. And it all begins with a taste of the finest wine—*taste and see* that the Lord is good and that the kingdom is here in the coming of Jesus. Let's keep moving through the narrative as we consider these tastes of the kingdom.

I Am the Bread of Life

We have already inspected the feeding of the multitudes in the Synoptics, noting how John also includes this scene in his Gospel (John 6). Here let's look at how John uniquely tells us what happens the very next day, when the crowd follows Jesus to an entirely different location. Apparently, they want more—but is it more of Jesus or more of the literal bread he provided? Jesus turns their seeking into a teaching moment, urging them to pursue the kind of bread that doesn't spoil, inviting them to believe in the one whom God sent. Now, one would think that this invitation would go over well. But the people are not convinced, and they ask Jesus for a sign to prove himself. They challenge Jesus to provide manna, just as Moses did for their ancestors in the wilderness. Jesus doesn't point out that he already did this on the previous day, but he corrects their understanding: "It is not *Moses* who has given you bread from heaven, but it is *my Father* who gives you *true* bread from heaven" (6:32). Jesus goes on to claim, "I am the bread of life. Whoever comes to me will never go hungry, and whoever believes in me will never be thirsty" (6:35). Well, this prompts all sorts of grumbling. The people are starting to resemble the hangry Israelites, grumbling at Moses in the wilderness.

Jesus strengthens this connection to their ancestors when he says, "Your ancestors ate the manna in the wilderness, and they died. . . . I am the living bread that came down from heaven. Whoever eats of *this* bread will live forever." If that wasn't shocking enough, Jesus gives the metaphor a little twist, adding, "And the bread that I will give for the life of the world is my *flesh*" (6:49, 51 NRSVue). Well, this sends the Jewish crowd to the next level of dismay: they go from grumbling to disgruntled wonder. *How can this be?* They cannot wrap their minds around the implications of Jesus's statement. And

Jesus doesn't let up, but presses in further: "Unless you eat the flesh of the Son of Man and drink his blood, you have no life in you" (6:53). And then he personalizes it: "Those who eat *my* flesh and drink *my* blood have eternal life" (6:54).

Well, by now the crowd's grumbling has become arguing, and it must involve a grappling with the incongruities they are feeling in their guts. Here is Jesus, who has healed their sick and provided bread to their hungry children. They want to stay with him, but at what cost? What does Jesus mean by "eat my flesh"?

For those who *want* to believe Jesus, they might be remembering that this whole conversation is taking place during Passover season, one of the great pilgrimage feasts. Every year, the Jewish community sets aside a week and gathers to worship and celebrate God's deliverance of their ancestors from enslavement in Egypt. Imagine how this annual commemoration would involve the sights, sounds, and smells of priests slaughtering, flaying, and then eating animal flesh, given for the purification of the people. Much like modern-day memories triggered for some at the mention of a holiday like Christmas, Jewish celebrants would remember the fellowship of a shared meal. They would eat the flesh of the Passover lamb, the unleavened bread, and the bitter herbs, and they would drink wine. All these activities form positive, nostalgic memories among those earnestly following God in yearly rhythms of worship. These memories are the result of habituated actions lodged deep into participants' bodies. The implications of Jesus's invitation—"whoever eats my flesh"—strike a buzz in the crowd. Those recalling Passover might reason that Jesus has to be referencing this holiday! But while it stokes intrigue, they can't quite make out its significance: Does "flesh" here have some sort of sacrificial connotation? How does this work? What does this mean?

Any receptivity and genuine interest will immediately clash with the negative hues in Jesus's words. Those in the crowd who want to protest are experiencing an opposite, visceral reaction for probably two different reasons. First, there are those who might associate eating flesh with cannibalism. Any connection to this barbaric, foreign practice would create understandable repulsion. Cannibalism was regarded as a primitive, immoral, and violent act, played out in only the most dire, dreadful conditions, such as war or famine. While most in the crowd would not have experiential memories of engaging in or even witnessing this practice, their understanding of it through hearsay of other cultures and past generations would negatively resound in their imaginations upon hearing Jesus's words.

By this point, if there were any lingering positive connections to flesh-eating, these would sour upon grappling with the second reason for protest: for a Jewish population, the off-limits notion of drinking blood. This prohibition would be deeply embedded into Jewish bodies since it was their cardinal belief that the life was in the blood (e.g., Lev. 17:11). Priests were trained to expertly drain the blood completely from sacrificial animals. So, the crowd considers Jesus's invitation with pessimism: *Whoever drinks my blood?* Whatever Jesus is implying here, it can't be good.

The shock of Jesus's claim, "I am the bread of life," and his invitation, "Whoever eats my flesh and drinks my blood has eternal life," proves to be too much for most who are present. Many are so disgruntled, in fact, that they walk away. I think that in part they protest because this is a messianic claim, and Jesus is suggesting salvation through a new kind of sacrifice involving a new way of engaging with God. They approach God through animal sacrifice and commemorative festivals and must contend with Jesus's invitation. He is asking them to take their foundational, habitual rhythms and map them onto himself. Can they refresh their former notions of what it looks like to relate to God? Once upon a time, the Father rained down manna from heaven for Israel. In the fullness of time, the Father sent Jesus to be the living manna from heaven. The invitation is to consider how consuming Jesus is salvific, akin to how the manna from heaven fed the Israelites when they were desperately hungry and dependent on this provision for survival.

Now, we are not being invited to eat actual flesh and drink actual blood. Jesus is clarifying something important about what saves us, and this salvation is framed as a kind of ingestion leading to nourishment. And somehow, death is an avenue to life. Jesus's flesh and blood represent sacrifice, and our ingestion of him is our true nourishment. Jesus's words have sacrificial "flavors" to them, and our taste, our consumption of him, leads to life.

The Hunger of the Earliest Readers

The earliest ancient readers of these Gospel narratives had an advantage over the crowds within the story because they were privy to the narration in the text. While they could make some of the same positive and negative connections as the crowd does about banquets, bread, fish, and wine, they (as we) were also postresurrection readers.[22] This means that they had the advantage of approaching Jesus's words retrospectively, viewing these scenes from the end of the narrative and putting the pieces together from there. Therefore, for example, Jesus equating himself to flesh that we must eat might not have sounded as foreign or offensive since earlier in the narrative John presents Jesus as the word made flesh (John 1:14), and he is the Lamb of God who takes away the sin of the world (1:29). Jesus's invitation to eat his flesh easily connects to the notion of Jesus sacrificially dying to give his flesh and blood on behalf of the world.

At the same time, however, ancient readers were not uniformly Jewish, and their reading of Jesus's words might have activated different experiential associations. For example, ancient readers occupying a post–AD 70, temple-less, diaspora setting might no longer have been prompted to make the same kinds of connections to Jewish practices centered on the temple, such as festivals like Passover.

A gentile readership located in the wider Greco-Roman world might have heard these stories about feasts, bread, flesh, and blood in a different register. For example, feasts and communal meals might have connected more closely to how gentile Greco-Roman communities feasted.[23] How might ancient readers have heard stories about Jesus's radical inclusiveness at the banquet table and let this reform their own banqueting practices as a result?

Jesus *as* bread might at first have resembled the inviting quality of physical sustenance, but there could also have been the knee-jerk

22. And it might be worth adding that the narrative is written from a postresurrection perspective. The difference that I am highlighting here is the perspective of the characters *within* the narrative world compared to the perspective of ancient readers. There is far less historical distance between these two groups than we have as modern readers. But there is still a distinct variation in perspective to account for between them.

23. Much has been studied about the banqueting practices of the early Christian world. See, for example, D. Smith, *From Symposium to Eucharist.*

repulsion to "flesh-eating" as cannibalism. At the same time, eating flesh and drinking blood could find a resting place within the context of eucharistic practices. Complicating this imagery would have been the way accusations of cannibalism were leveled against the early churches throughout the Roman Empire because of their practice of the Eucharist. It is interesting to consider how misperceptions of the Eucharist might have stained the reputation of the early church. Did reading Jesus's invitation to eat flesh and drink blood incite further division between followers of Jesus and all others? How would these words have been received in local synagogues, where there were still Jewish followers of Jesus participating in regular worship? Amid such tensions, within the complexities (and hardships) of being associated with a countercultural movement, perhaps the picture of the eschatological feast would have served as an encouragement to those celebrating Eucharist with the desire to mimic God's heart for all those in attendance.

Hunger and Thirst of Modern Readers

Have you ever eaten a memorable meal and talked about it for weeks afterward? Do certain foods carry so much significance that they are served only on important occasions? What kinds of routines do you have in your life involving certain foods? Coffee is for first thing in the morning, vegetable stew is for dreary winter days, garlic mashed potatoes are only at grandma's dinner table, and baked-from-scratch red velvet birthday cake is so decadent that we eat it only once a year. We have habits and rote practices around foods that nourish us and that call to mind certain seasons, people, joys, and sorrows in our lives.

In this tasting tour through the Gospels, we have watched Jesus compare the kingdom of God to an extravagant dinner party where all are welcome. God is the compassionate, generous host, and he serves the finest food and drink, that all might enjoy this joyous union together. Jesus plays host when he embodies this generosity in remote places, feeding people who need hope and a filling meal. And ultimately, Jesus claims to be the very bread of life that we consume to find true and lasting nourishment.

As we continue to "chew" on Jesus's invitation to the banquet table, can these ingestion metaphors teach us something about the *quality* of our interaction with Jesus? Let's reflect on our physical lives of eating and drinking. Think about how we interact with food and drink to stay alive: we do so daily and continually. Our relationship to sustenance is not a one-and-done, all-you-can-eat buffet that sustains us for a lifetime. Instead, we eat and drink routinely, habitually, waking up each day with new caloric needs. This is a dynamic existence, one that manifests a continual dependence on nutrients for survival. This loops us back to our opening question: Have you ever been hungry? Sure, every day. We wake up with the need to eat and drink, and our hunger goes away with each meal, but then it returns. In other words, we will never outgrow our dependence on nutrients.

This might push against our instincts—to say that we will be forever dependent. In the modern, well-fed, individualistic waters in which we swim, the tide flows in the direction of independence. We raise our up-and-coming generations to develop into self-sufficient, autonomous human beings who can take care of themselves. It therefore can be easy for our hearts to default to search for the kind of peace fueled by our individual, internal reserves. We find comfort when we can control the fortifications that we have constructed around us. We are accustomed to an "I can do it myself because I'm capable" approach to life. We never want to put others out. Or maybe we don't want to appear weak.

It's only when we are confronted with threats to our independence—whether through sickness, economic challenge, physical or relational loss, or mental-emotional-psychological pain—that our equilibrium is thrown off. Such challenges force us into a dependence that feels unnatural and is mostly countercultural. We often respond by pushing against our dependency—we seek relief from it; we want it to end; we don't find "peace" until our internal reserves of self-sufficiency are restored. These are the times when we let others into our need—when we are desperate, when our resources are depleted. But we always hope that it's temporary.

But what if it's this sense of dependence that is key to our hunger for Jesus? What if the ideal posture for finding Jesus is when we are most in touch with our dependence, vulnerability, and need? Those who recognize their hunger are the ones who tend to clamor for the next meal, to gather the manna from the ground, and to hang on Jesus's every word and follow him no matter what. I worry about living such a life where I endlessly and unthinkingly invest my energies into my own self-sufficiency and autonomy. How might this inhibit me from knowing my hunger and my need for Jesus the living bread? How does my independence lull me into this notion that I have control, and how does this set my heart into a posture that holds Jesus at arm's length? *I'm good. I've got this!* It's the same message we tell our friends and neighbors: *Don't worry about me, Jesus. I'll let you know when I really need you.* We end up saving Jesus for emergencies. But we need food every day.

As we consider Jesus as the living bread whose once-for-all sacrifice of flesh and blood sustains us into eternity, can we also consider how this union with him is continuous and ongoing? This is exactly how we see this play out in Scripture. Day after day God rained down manna from heaven to feed his people in the wilderness. Jesus similarly provided a feast for a crowd, and he did so with compassion and welcome. And he also offers himself as the meal: "Those who eat my flesh and drink my blood abide in me and I in them" (John 6:56 NRSVue). This sounds to me like a constant interaction, one that never ends. It's marked by welcome, ongoing presence, sustenance, and meeting continual need. We are never without him.

TASTY BITES
FOR FURTHER NOURISHMENT

1. Have you ever been hungry? Consider engaging in a food fast. If you have never fasted before, an easy way to start is to eat a good lunch and then go all the way until lunchtime the next day. This means that you skip only two meals—dinner, breakfast—and then you can break your fast with lunch. (Be sure to stay hydrated!) During your fast, every time you feel hungry, turn your attention to Jesus, even with a simple prayer. Consider using your mealtime to

read and meditate on his Word. Finally, during *and after* your fast, reflect on what hunger felt like. Did it make you feel weak? Did it make you feel your dependence? What kinds of emotions were brought up? What might God show you through your hunger?

2. Jesus claims to be the bread of life, but sometimes we fill our stomachs with "snacks" that take away from our hunger for Jesus. Consider lining up five snacks you love to eat. For five days in a row, as you enjoy one of these snacks, reflect: How might these get in the way of your main meal? For each day, reflect on one kind of "snack" that you consume in your life more broadly that keeps you satiated enough to not realize your need for Christ. Are there ways that you can put off your dependence on these "snacks" in order to be hungry for the main meal?

3. Have you ever hosted a banquet? What would it look like to extend the hospitality of God by inviting friends and/or acquaintances into your space to enjoy fellowship over a meal? It can be as simple or as elaborate as you can afford, and to minimize or share the work, consider inviting others to contribute their favorite dish to share. Come to your meal prepared to share life with one another. For example, are there preset questions you can initiate as part of your meal conversation? It can be a mixture of lighthearted topics and questions to invite greater depth. Observe how sharing a meal together articulates value and friendship to everyone who participates.

4

Seeing and Not Seeing

Jesus, the Light and the Giver of Sight

Earlier this year my husband woke up experiencing blurred vision in his right eye. Thinking he had wrongly placed his contact lenses, he switched them, and then he turned them inside out and back again, but nothing helped. The ophthalmologist confirmed a retinal detachment with a "giant" tear (that was the official wording on the medical chart). Surgery was needed, and urgently, so that the detachment would not become permanent. The procedure involved injecting a gas bubble into his eye to stimulate reattachment; as a result, his vision was restored, but it didn't return fully for several weeks.

It can be easy to take for granted certain embodied capacities. It's only when a sensory ability goes missing—such as vision, even partially—that we realize how much we rely on it. During this season when he had use of only one eye, Garrick was repeatedly confronted with how much he had relied on two. When I would walk into a room where the door was on his right side, he often did not realize I was there. Thinking I was upstairs, he would call out for me, and I would calmly say, "Honey, I'm right here." We have marveled at the technology that masterminded this retinal repair; it was all in a day's work for his surgeon. In less than an hour she turned a malady that would have been permanently life-altering not too many years ago into a brief pause in his use of both eyes.

In this chapter we turn our attention to the sense of sight and how it materializes in the biblical world, the Gospel texts, and our own lives as we engage Scripture. Like all the other physical senses, the sense of sight is a good gift from the Lord, helping us to perceive his work in the world. As you might recall from chapter 1, sight lives at the top of the sensory hierarchy in today's context. This preeminence gives sight a level of complexity that we will unpack shortly. For example, we often use visual language to designate knowledge, understanding, and faith. Scripture does this too. Blindness, therefore, is frequently a negative portrait of the opposite. What are the implications of this persistent negative portrayal of blindness for those with visual deficits? How can we understand this dynamic alongside Jesus giving sight to the blind throughout the Gospels? Before we get to the Gospel texts, the following will discuss how sight operates, along with the role it plays in both ancient and modern contexts.

Insights on Sight

One of the potential effects of being sighted in a sight-centric world is the temptation to overlook what sight can offer our approach to "engaging Jesus with our senses." Sight is so much a part of our lives that we can be rather unreflective about it. For the sighted, our eyes are much like the water a fish swims in. Have you ever given much thought about how much you rely on your eyes for your daily routines, like navigating your way to the kitchen for some coffee or for styling your hair each morning? Have you ever thought about how much you utilize your eyes in engaging with God? We use our eyes to read Scripture or to pen words into a journal or type into a device. Our eyes help us marvel at the sights of God's creation, and I suspect that we tend to focus more on the beauty of creation than the fact that we can see it.

The Anatomy of Sight

In Aristotle's exploration of the senses, he observes the media involved in the actual physical operation of each sense. The sense of sight, he noticed, functions as an indirect process: the medium of air conducts color to the eye, which sees.[1] This means that sight operates in a distanced fashion. We don't enact sight by placing an object in direct contact with the eye. This is a fairly big contrast with senses like taste or touch, whose literal operations are direct and intimate. Consequently, we can view a lot of objects and remain completely distant from them, while to touch something requires us to get very close. This literal distance of sight within a sight-centric society plays a role in its high rank.[2] Our modern Western penchant for scientific verification leads us to value detached objectivity along with rationality and the ability to categorize things in an orderly fashion. These values are instilled from a young age. Many years ago, J. C. Carothers observed how visually focused cultures in the West fostered learning alongside African communities that prioritized hearing over sight. In the West, we foster a child's development using visual play, with colorful blocks or by putting big plastic keys in locks. This trains a child to think in particular ways, with a focus on "spatio-temporal relations."[3] By contrast, he observed African communities whose education was directed more toward spoken word with an embedded quality of drama and emotion. Here the senses were more overlapped and mixed together in communication.[4] Based on this, it appears that the anatomy of sight and its premier position in a cultural context promote particular ways of interacting with the world.

Sight in Modern and Ancient Contexts

As we prepare to explore its presence in the Gospels, it's helpful to consider how sight operates in both modern and ancient contexts;

1. Aristotle (*On the Soul* 2.419a10) states, "Colour moves the transparent medium, e.g., the air, and this, being continuous, acts upon the sense organ."
2. Howes and Classen (*Ways of Sensing*, 8) emphasize how the physical operations of the senses are relevant to their placement within hierarchies.
3. McLuhan ("Five Sense Sensorium," 44–45) presents Carothers's 1959 research to demonstrate the differences between cultures focused on oral/aural contexts and those focused on spatio-visual contexts.
4. McLuhan, "Five Sense Sensorium," 45.

there are similarities and differences. One of the primary similarities is that both eras seem to reflect a sensory hierarchy wherein sight is preeminent. To lose visual capacity would be life-altering in both contexts, but these scenarios look different from each other.

One of the most significant factors relevant for these differing pictures of sight in the ancient and modern worlds has got to be technology. In many ways our modern technologies *foster* the preeminence of sight by reinforcing our reliance on it. Consider the proliferation of our dependence on screens—whether television, computers, tablets, gaming devices, or smartphones. This reliance ushers in greater dependence on our eyes, which over time perhaps produces higher instances of eye problems caused by overuse, such as visual deficits and migraine headaches (or detached retinas).[5] But not to worry: alongside this increased dependence on our eyes we have technologies aimed at lessening the ill effects of our eye diseases and visual impairments. Not only can we reattach retinas but we can eradicate cataracts and employ laser technology to correct nearsightedness. Extending even further back, for hundreds of years we have had the simple technology of eyeglasses, which help us navigate our sight-centric worlds. So yes, we are relying on our eyes more than ever, but with this are many resources to help prolong vision for larger populations of people.

None of these technologies would have been a feature of the ancient world. While sight was significant in the first century, there was probably less eyestrain because sight was not employed to the same extent. However, think about how much more challenging it would have been for someone experiencing simple nearsightedness. There was far less that could be done to help: not only were there no retinal specialists but there were no contact lenses or glasses, not to mention all the assistive technologies we have available today for those with substantial visual impairments. I hope that this discussion raises our awareness of how sight operates in our world but also how critical it would have been for those in the ancient world.

5. E.g., see Ayesha Rascoe and Hadeel Al-Shalchi, "Why Myopia Is Becoming Increasingly Common among Kids and Adults," *Weekend Edition Sunday*, NPR (website), July 23, 2023, https://www.npr.org/2023/07/23/1189659924/why-myopia-is-becoming-increasingly-common-among-kids-and-adults.

Sight and Blindness in Scripture

When talking about sense perception, we inevitably confront the reality that not everyone possesses the same configuration of sensory abilities, and in fact many walk through life with one ability that is partial or missing. The effect of this deficit is compounded when that missing capacity is so dominant in culture that society is shaped around its use. As we have begun to "see," sight is one of these abilities.[6] The predominance of sight makes it easy for those who don't have it to feel and be sidelined.

What an important gift it is, then, to learn from those experiencing blindness as we explore sight in the Gospels. To that end, I'd like to introduce you to the work of John Hull (1935–2015), who was professor of religious education at the University of Birmingham. As a young man, Hull gradually lost his vision completely due to cataracts and retinal detachments, and he went on to contribute important reflections not only on how he processed this loss but also on his experience of blindness in a sighted world and, significantly, as he interacted with Scripture. He introduces his masterful *In the Beginning There Was Darkness* by addressing how Scripture excludes those who are blind, starting at the beginning with "and God saw that the light was good" (Gen. 1:4). He writes,

> God pronounces as good something that means nothing to those who are totally blind, and that is a source of longing and frustration, perhaps even despair, for those who still have a little sight. Here we come upon one of the great stumbling blocks that the Bible places in the way of blind people. It speaks of values that, for them, cannot be values. It announces that God is on the side of, and has a preference for, a world that is not their world—a reality to which they have no access.[7]

Whoa! I hadn't thought of that perspective before I first read it. Hull goes on to describe the hardship it is for those with visual deficits

---

6. Hearing is another one of these predominant senses, which we will address in the next chapter. We cannot really do justice here to all we can learn from one another based on our varying collections of personal sensory capacities.

7. Hull, *In the Beginning*, 2.

to be persistently portrayed in Scripture as the negative example of unbelief. Sure enough, Scripture does this. A lot. Hull doesn't mince words, advising blind and partially sighted readers to remember that it was written by and for sighted people, stating, "It is just the way that it was unconsciously adapted by the sighted people who wrote it."[8] He is perhaps not wrong. Bethany McKinney Fox conducts an important conversation with other interpreters in the disability community to remind us that those without disabilities "are inherently biased against disability. This bias exists because 'non-disabled people take their experiences of the world as normal, thereby marginalizing and excluding the experiences of people with disabilities as not normal.'"[9]

While much of this feels like an indictment against a sighted world (and a sighted God), this isn't the whole story. Since God looks beyond appearances to the heart (1 Sam. 16:7), Hull observes how God is beyond both sight and blindness.[10] He traces some ways that blindness can be an avenue to draw close to God, and I am eager to integrate his reflections into our discussion of sight in Scripture.[11]

Yael Avrahami provides detailed discussion of all the ways sight language is used throughout the Hebrew Bible, which is worth summarizing here because of how steeped in Scripture the Gospel writers and some of the earliest readers were. She begins by noting that God created the senses, has sensory ability (Gen. 1:31), and is the sole source of all sensory ability (Exod. 4:11; Pss. 94:9; 146:8; Isa. 35:5–6; 42:7). By contrast, idols are explicitly unable to sense at all (Deut. 4:28; Ps. 115:2–8).[12] Divine punishment is frequently expressed through damage to the senses, especially sight, inflicted on those opposed to God's people (Gen. 19:11), on Israel's enemies in battle (2 Kings 6:18–19), on Israelites who are disobedient (Deut.

8. Hull, *In the Beginning*, 67.
9. Fox, *Disability*, 93, quoting Yong, *Bible, Disability*, 67. Both of these resources are excellent, and the reader would do well to check them out.
10. Hull, *In the Beginning*, 75–76.
11. This is a complex conversation. It requires the utmost sensitivity to the diversity of ways we understand and navigate varying collections of sensory abilities. I acknowledge that the following discussion may have some shortcomings, and I remain open to learning how to converse about it better.
12. Avrahami, *Senses of Scripture*, 190–92.

28:28–29), and through human punishment (Judg. 16:21; 2 Kings 25:7).[13]

The Old Testament Scriptures present those with (sensory and other) disabilities in a couple of ways. First, people with disabilities appear to be hindered in their ability to earn a living, which would essentially cast them out to the margins of their community.[14] Someone who was blind would have been considered among the marginalized, along with the alien, widow, and orphan. They were dependent on their community to survive, and Israel was instructed to care for and treat them justly (Lev. 19:13–15; Deut. 27:18–19; Prov. 31:8–9).[15] Second, those with sensory disabilities were viewed negatively because of the perception that sensory damage was the result of divine judgment.[16] From there developed a tendency to link their sensory deficit to short-falls in other areas, deeming them inferior in knowledge, or in morality (they were regarded as sinners), or in wisdom (they were regarded as fools [e.g., Jer. 5:21]).[17] Let's unpack this tendency a bit more.

Recall from chapter 1 the discussion about how in today's world sight (along with hearing) is often allied with philosophical reflection and knowledge. Sight language is so prevalent, in fact, that it is embedded into our language today when we speak about gaining understanding and knowledge. "See?" is often a question that means, "Do you *understand* what I mean?" This dynamic also shows up in the words of Scripture. One only has to recall the psalmist's memorable invitation to "taste and *see* that the Lord is good" (Ps. 34:8) to notice how in this case both tasting and seeing are being used symbolically to connote a kind of experiential knowledge.[18]

13. Avrahami, *Senses of Scripture*, 196–201. She goes on to summarize how damage to the senses was customary especially in war for two purposes: to weaken one side's position and "to create moral damage to the vanquished." This ultimately conveys that "loss in war is divine rejection" (202). Finally, sensory impairment (especially sight but also hearing and taste) also occurs in Scripture with old age (202–3).

14. Avrahami, *Senses of Scripture*, 206.

15. Avrahami, *Senses of Scripture*, 207.

16. Avrahami, *Senses of Scripture*, 207.

17. Avrahami, *Senses of Scripture*, 212–13. She recognizes the associative pattern created by these repeated associations, which links together foolishness, sin, deafness, and blindness.

18. It probably suggests something more like "experience and know" the Lord's goodness.

If seeing is equivalent to knowledge, understanding, and even faith, the opposite is applied to lack of sight. Hull points out how distressing it is as a blind person to encounter blindness used as a metaphor for sin, corruption, and wickedness.[19] Speaking about Israel rejecting Jesus as Messiah, the Gospel writers draw on Isaiah for one of the most memorable examples: "Be ever hearing, but never understanding; be ever seeing, but never perceiving. Make the heart of this people calloused; make their ears dull and close their eyes. Otherwise they might see with their eyes, hear with their ears, understand with their hearts, and turn and be healed" (Isa. 6:9–10; see Matt. 13:14–15; Mark 4:11–12; Luke 8:10; John 12:40).[20] Notice how being blind and deaf are metaphors for unbelief and lack of understanding.

This mindset seems to be embedded in the world of the Gospels, as evidenced by the question Jesus's disciples ask Jesus in John 9:2: "Rabbi, who sinned, this man or his parents, that he was born blind?" Thankfully, Jesus's answer is, "Neither." As New Testament scholar Jaime Clark-Soles says of this interaction, this is a bad question to begin with since "not all suffering has the same source, quality, quantity, degree or 'solution.'"[21] And yet, based on what we have observed about the Old Testament's presentation of blindness, we can understand how Jesus's disciples might operate with such a mindset. Blindness does seem to be cast negatively, frequently connected with sin and a lack of God's favor.

This is troubling to the degree that this carries into the church today, as we ourselves are prone to associate blindness with a lack of knowledge, faith, or understanding. Fox describes the common perception of people with disabilities as being helpless and passive, lacking God's presence "until non-disabled people bring it to them."[22] People with disabilities frequently report being approached by well-

---

19. Hull, *In the Beginning*, 95. He traces the origin of this mindset to sighted people watching a blind person in public use their hands in order to help their feet to find the path to walk (96). This slower and "groping" pace resembles people who have "morally lost their way, whose path is devious."

20. For fuller discussion, see Hull, *In the Beginning*, 97–100.

21. Clark-Soles, *Reading John*, 48.

22. Fox, *Disability*, 99.

meaning Christians who want to pray for their healing. Unfortunately, sometimes the pray-er assumes that a person's persistent disability is connected to a lack of faith in God or a lack of favor from God. Other times the pray-er falsely assumes that what this person most wants prayer for is restoration of their sight.

In the Gospels Jesus frequently brought sight to the blind. It's the basis for our impulse to ask God to restore sight to those who have visual deficits today. Seeking after and celebrating the ability to see seems to be an extension of God's visible world, designed to be engaged in part through our visual abilities. But Jesus didn't always assume that this was what someone wanted, as he asks one blind man, "What do you want me to do for you?" (Mark 10:51; Luke 18:41; cf. Matt. 20:32). Hull highlights the importance of this question, which ascribes to this man agency to make his request. Hull wryly supposes that "nowadays, the blind person would have said, 'Get me some computer training and a job with a firm which has a decent equal opportunities policy.'"[23]

Hull's insights remind us of the complexity of the matter. He states, "There is a sense in which the advantages of sight are so obvious that no one would prefer to be blind."[24] Hull even supposes that one never loses the fantasy of having their sight fully restored.[25] But amid the reality of his persistent blindness he describes reaching a place where his blindness was no longer an "affliction" to him. Instead, it became for him "a strange, dark and mysterious gift from God." While he states that he would not wish it on anyone, nor was he happy to receive it, through blindness he encountered God in a new way. He considered himself to have passed "beyond light and darkness," where God dwells (Ps. 139:12). No sighted person can claim this experience.[26]

---

23. Hull, *In the Beginning*, 44.
24. Hull, *In the Beginning*, 45, adding that "the advantages of having two legs are so obvious that no one would prefer to have one leg or none" and "the advantages of being loved are so obvious that [no one] would prefer to be unloved."
25. Hull, *In the Beginning*, 45–46, adding, "It is on that fantasy that the would-be faith healer exercises his manipulative power," recalling his encounters with such people.
26. Hull (*In the Beginning*, 48) follows this up by stating, "In that respect it seems to me that it is blind people who are in the image of God rather than sighted people."

Just as Jesus instructs Peter not to compare his path to that of his fellow disciple (John 21:20–23), Hull reminds us that each of us walks our own road of discipleship.[27] As we turn now to review the presence of sight in the Gospels, let's continue to reflect on the diversity of ways sight and blindness figure into our relationships with God and our abilities to engage Jesus with our senses.

Sight in the Synoptics

From the very outset of the Gospels, the sense of sight is employed to talk about Jesus's messianic vocation. The Gospel writers draw heavily on the prophet Isaiah, whose figurative use of sight reminds the sighted of how light dispels darkness in their world. Just as a plant requires sunlight to grow, light represents flourishing for those who depend on their eyes to get around. Wherever darkness represents fear, uncertainty, and even death, the light eradicates these properties from one's surroundings.

And All People Will See God's Salvation

Luke positions John the Baptizer as the witness to God's coming redemption; he is "a voice of one calling in the wilderness" (Luke 3:4a). John's words recall Isaiah speaking to the Israelites, who are anticipating God's return to Zion.[28] John's message to the crowds in Jesus's day is that they are to "prepare the way for the Lord, make straight paths for him" (3:4b),[29] and Luke adds that all people will *see* the salvation of God (Luke 3:6 // Isa. 40:5). This resonates with Simeon's joyful prayer to God over the infant Jesus: "My eyes have *seen* your salvation, which you have prepared *in the sight of* all nations: a *light* for revelation to the Gentiles, and the glory of your people Israel" (Luke 2:30–32).[30] Jesus is the embodied, visible manifestation of God. In him we *see* the kingdom of God come to earth.

27. Hull, *In the Beginning*, 163–64.
28. Chen, *Luke*, 48.
29. See Luke 3:4b–5 // Isa. 40:3–4; cf. Matt. 3:3b; Mark 1:3.
30. Chen (*Luke*, 48) notices this connection.

The People Living in Darkness Have Seen a Great Light

After Jesus is tested in the wilderness, he is ready to begin his ministry. Matthew likewise interprets Jesus's coming as fulfilling Isaiah's words and ushering in the kingdom of heaven (Matt. 4:17): "The people living in darkness have *seen a great light*; on these living in the land of the shadow of death *a light has dawned*" (Matt. 4:16 // Isa. 9:2). Notice again the figurative light and darkness, where darkness represents those in "dire straits," and deliverance—God's saving work—is characterized as a great *light*.[31]

It is no accident that Matthew narrates Jesus's relocation to Capernaum (Matt. 4:13). Jesus is living in the same region of Zebulun and Naphtali that Isaiah mentions (Matt. 4:15 // Isa. 9:1), which recalls the "political darkness" that Israel faced under the threat of Assyria. In Jesus's day Capernaum is a Galilean town inhabited by a mix of Jews and gentiles. Capernaum is likely an object of disdain for the more "enlightened" religious establishment in Jerusalem.[32] But because Jesus is residing in Capernaum, he is poised to bring the *light* of God's kingdom to *all* nations (Matt. 28:18–20).[33]

Anointed to Restore

Let's address one more passage introducing Jesus's messianic vocation: Luke 4:18, quoting Isaiah 61:1. Here Jesus *himself* presents his ministry within the Isaianic stream. On a visit to his hometown of Nazareth, Jesus gets up to speak at a Sabbath synagogue gathering. He basically proclaims that Isaiah's words have been fulfilled among them, as *he* is the one anointed by the Spirit of the Lord for a particular purpose.

One scholar notes that the Spirit of the Lord's anointing "gives shape to the messianic ministry of Jesus."[34] What is this shape? Jesus tells us: he has come to bring good news to the poor, to proclaim freedom for prisoners, to *recover sight for the blind*, and to set the oppressed free (Luke 4:18–19 // Isa. 61:1–2; cf. 58:6). With Jesus's arrival comes

---

31. Wegner, *Isaiah*, 121. The darkness is literally "the shadow of death."
32. Turner, *Matthew*, 133.
33. Turner, *Matthew*, 133–34.
34. Carroll, *Luke*, 112.

the kingdom of God, ushering in an abundant quality of restoration and reversal, not only effecting spiritual change but also transforming material, physical, and social realities. Jesus "sets the oppressed free" through forgiveness,[35] and he embodies compassion to all. This will be particularly significant for those on the margins, which includes not only the materially poor but *anyone* of low status who tends to be overlooked and who is unable to reciprocate (see also Luke 14:13).[36]

One of the ways Jesus embodies Isaiah's words is by bringing actual physical reversals to people's lives through healing. As Jesus restores sight to those who are blind, he is fulfilling this messianic vocation that he initiates here.

Jesus Gives Sight to the Blind

There are several overlapping accounts of how Jesus brings sight to those who are blind. As we trace the ins and outs of several interactions, think about the significance of an individual regaining sight: this is an incredible reversal. No doubt this would introduce the joys surrounding sight—the ability to see one's loved ones, to see nature, birds, the sky, along with the capacity to walk by sight along a populated path. This would also carry significant social and economic implications for that person.

Our first example illustrates this dynamic. Known in Mark's Gospel as Bartimaeus (10:46–52), this man is described as blind and begging by the roadside. In the absence of a social welfare system or family wealth, this was probably one of the few options he had for supporting himself.[37] His story also appears in Matthew (20:29–34) and Luke (18:35–43), although Luke's man is unnamed, while Matthew reports two men.[38] In all three accounts the man is sitting along

35. Green, *Luke*, 211.
36. Chen (*Luke*, 61) elaborates that those considered of low status include children, barren women, widows, gentiles, tax collectors, sinners, the demon-possessed, those with physical deformities and sickness, and those with moral or ritual impurities. Green (*Luke*, 211) notes that it depends on a number of factors, such as education, gender, family heritage, religious purity, vocation, and economics.
37. Strauss, *Mark*, 468.
38. Matthew could be narrating a different tradition about two blind men. Strauss (*Mark*, 468n6) mentions that perhaps Mark focuses only on the one who ended

the bustling road going out of Jericho. When he hears that Jesus is passing by, he shouts, "Jesus, Son of David, have mercy on me!" The crowd rebukes him as a nuisance,[39] perhaps because this shouting was startling, an inappropriate show of emotion.[40] Unfazed, Bartimaeus keeps calling out to Jesus. Maybe he is accustomed to being shushed. But maybe his persistence was fueled by his weariness at having known a "lifetime of indignities" coupled with what he had heard about and hoped for in Jesus.[41]

Jesus stops and calls him over. What happens next is remarkable. I mentioned this earlier, but think of the way Jesus dignifies this man by asking him, "What would you like me to do for you?" Jesus doesn't assume anything. Hull observes how this question grants the man independence and demonstrates "gracious acceptance."[42] I'll bet that Bartimaeus hasn't experienced these qualities very often, always dependent on others and yet never fully welcomed by them.

Jesus gives sight to Bartimaeus. He affirms his faith as the catalyst: "Your faith has healed you." But in Mark and Luke the text can be literally translated, "Your faith has *saved* you."[43] This speaks to a sort of deliverance from affliction,[44] a release from suffering that I'm guessing has something to do with Bartimaeus's place in society. His blindness has forced him into a dependence on others for charity in order to get by, and probably he is unable to offer much in return. As such, he would be considered "expendable."[45]

Within this faith declaration Hull highlights Jesus's exhortation to Bartimaeus, "Go." As sighted readers, we might skip over that little word. I did. But one could read it as "Go your way" (RSV).

---

up following Jesus. Note also how Matthew mentions two demoniacs (8:28–34) to Mark's one (5:1–17).

39. Evans, *Mark 8:27–16:20*, 130.

40. Hull, *In the Beginning*, 43.

41. Evans, *Mark 8:27–16:20*, 133.

42. Hull, *In the Beginning*, 44.

43. Jesus uses the same language when he heals the woman with the hemorrhage: "Your faith has saved you" (Mark 5:34).

44. Evans, *Mark 8:27–16:20*, 134.

45. Green (*Luke*, 663) notes that his place among "the poor" means that his existence was potentially recognized only by those who valued Jewish almsgiving.

Hull notices how this suggests a totally new life for this man. Now he actually *can* go his way. Bartimaeus was accustomed to a level of dependence that he would no longer need. This is quite a shift into a new way of life altogether. Notice, what did Bartimaeus choose to do in response to Jesus's call to "go"? He follows Jesus.[46]

Some have interpreted this restoration of sight as symbolic for coming to faith and understanding.[47] Mark narrates another such time in Bethsaida, when Jesus brings about a healing in two stages (8:22–26). The first time Jesus touches the man's eyes, his sight is partially restored: "I see people; they look like trees walking around" (8:24). After the second touch the man's sight is restored completely. This is often interpreted symbolically to represent the disciples' gradual spiritual understanding throughout Mark.[48]

To conclude our discussion of Jesus bringing sight to the blind, let's consider the *mode* of Jesus's healing of the man. Jesus often uses the sense of touch to enact sight.[49] There is an entire upcoming chapter devoted to touch, but for now let's recall the opposite anatomies of sight compared to touch: sight is rather indirect, while touch is direct. At other times Jesus restores sight with just a word, remaining at a physical distance, but touch introduces an interactive dynamic into these healings. Hull notices how Jesus takes this man by the hand to lead him out of the town (Mark 8:23), calling this "one of the most beautiful and moving incidents regarding

46. Hull (*In the Beginning*, 44) writes, "The way that Bartimaeus chooses is the way of discipleship."

47. Hull (*In the Beginning*, 44) reads this as a parable about conversion. Of course, he says, this symbol is from a sighted person's perspective: "To be delivered from the restrictions of blindness into the freedom of a sighted person's life is one of the most desirable transformations that a sighted person could imagine" (45).

48. Strauss, *Mark*, 351. Hull (*In the Beginning*, 41) adds that the disciples' full sight is restored once they experience the resurrection, ascension, and day of Pentecost. Beavis ("From the Margin to the Way") takes a different approach. She traces the role played by a blind seer in the ancient world, suggesting that we understand Bartimaeus against this background. This makes his words "Jesus, Son of David" to be a prophetic, inspired declaration (37). Ultimately, for her, Bartimaeus is a figure to be admired for his prophetic role.

49. He doesn't always use touch. Note how he is not narrated as touching Bartimaeus in Mark 10 or in the parallel account in Luke 18. But Matthew narrates that he does (20:34). He also uses touch to enact sight in Matt. 9:27–31 and Mark 8:22–26.

blindness in the entire Bible."[50] It conveys a tangible level of support and intimacy.

And then, Jesus uses the lowest-ranked sense, touch—a sensory action highly regulated around ritual purity laws—and he gets right up close to the man to create the highest-ranked sense, sight. (He even uses his own saliva.)[51] Consider that for the blind man touch is probably more highly ranked in his own personal sensorium. He probably relies on touch more than most sighted people. I wonder how much Jesus is "speaking this man's language" by engaging him in such a familiar way. Jesus's use of touch makes this a very humble and intimate interaction. This is something worth reflecting on.

Hence, as we have "seen," one of the ways we know that Jesus is ushering in the kingdom of God is how he brings sight to those who are blind. The goodness of this gesture is not only in the joy at the physical reality for the individual but also in how it has the potential to restore someone to their community in full participation, as a way of healing injustice.[52]

The Goodness of Light for the Sighted

There is much more we could say about sight in the Synoptics. As we prepare to move to the Gospel of John, let's consider briefly how sight is closely related to the theme of light. For sighted communities, light is good. Light helps eyes to see in order to gain needed understanding. Jesus teaches that when you light a lamp, logically, you place it on a stand so others can see by its light. This tangible parable encourages Jesus's followers to share his teachings widely,

50. Hull, *In the Beginning*, 40.
51. Strauss, *Mark*, 322. We are not sure why Jesus uses spit to heal this man. He does this two other times in the Gospels (Mark 7:31–37; John 9:1–7). In the ancient world, saliva was often viewed as curative, having "magical" or healing properties. However, there were also negative connotations that could indicate shame or impurity (e.g., Num. 12:14).
52. Fox (*Disability*, 89–93) affirms and describes how interpreters mostly view such social inclusion as good, but she also highlights the difficulties some will have. For example, one interpretation understands Jesus as fixing bodies so they can "follow the rules," allowing these exclusionary practices to continue.

not to hide them away under a bowl or a bed.[53] Sight and light are analogous to getting the word out, to sharing good news.[54]

Another time, Jesus calls the eye the "lamp" of the body. If your eyes are healthy, your whole body will be full of light. But if your eyes are unhealthy, your whole body will be filled with darkness (Matt. 6:22–24; Luke 11:34–36). Many see evidence here of the ancient "extramission" view of sight, which understands the eyes as the source of light coming forth from the body. Moderns tend to take the "intromission" view of sight, where the eyes take in light. There is debate about which view was prevalent then and which is operative in this passage.[55] Regardless, this analogy highlights the ideal of cultivating wholeness and generosity in one's life as opposed to being greedy and envious.[56] Here we see how the goodness of sight can help the sighted to understand the merits of aligning oneself to God's kingdom values.

Sighted Oversights

Some final comments will complete our survey of sight in the Synoptics. Hull makes some helpful observations about Matthew's Sermon on the Mount. As he highlights the sight language throughout, he reminds those who use their eyes that we must take extra care when it comes to relying on appearances.

For example, we as followers of Jesus have a real problem with exacting judgment, which Jesus presents in visual terms: "Why do you look at the speck of sawdust in your brother's eye and pay no attention to the plank in your own eye?" (Matt. 7:3). Or what about lust, since "anyone who *looks* at a woman lustfully has already committed adultery with her in his heart" (5:28)? Or consider the warnings

---

53. Matt. 5:15–16; Mark 4:21–23; Luke 8:16–18; 11:33.

54. Note how in Mark and Luke the sight metaphor is a shift from *hearing* imagery, where the seed of the gospel is sown, and the soil is a measure of how well someone hears the word (e.g., Luke 8:15).

55. Dale Allison (Davies and Allison, *Matthew I–VII*, 635–41) conducts a thorough discussion of the matter, and Pennington (*Sermon on the Mount*, 240–42) provides a helpful interpretation. Here the healthy eye may also be contrasted with the ancient view of the "evil eye," associated with greed and envy.

56. Pennington, *Sermon on the Mount*, 242–43. He ties this to the wider context in Matthew of not storing up treasures in heaven, noting that Matt. 6:24 continues with not serving two masters, God and money.

against hypocrisy and those who "disfigure their faces to *show* others they are fasting" (6:16). Finally, think about how easy it is to submit to comparison and worry, as we are exhorted, "*Look* at the birds of the air. . . . Why do you worry about clothes?" (6:26a, 28a).

Now, it's true that these kinds of exhortations apply to both the sighted and nonsighted worlds. Hull highlights how Matthew uses other senses too—including taste and touch—to draw similar analogies. We are all prone to judgment, lust, hypocrisy, and worry. However, sight language reminds the sighted of how prone we are to superficiality and judging by appearance.[57] These visually framed exhortations *can* provide helpful caution for the sighted to not let our eyes lead to our downfall. This should give us pause as we consider how our eyes can lead us to stray *away* from God just as easily as they can help us draw near.

Sight in the Fourth Gospel

We don't get very far into the Fourth Gospel before we realize that John is a bit obsessed with light/dark contrasts, possibly mirroring the ancient world's tendency to ascribe light to goodness and darkness to evil.[58] All our previous discussion about how such language can be troubling for those with visual deficits must apply here as well. With that awareness lingering in the background, the following will seek to celebrate the goodness of sight for the sighted, recognizing that this must be held in tension with the pain of how darkness can be cast so negatively. Once again, there is much to learn from one another in the panoply of diversities in our multisensory lives.[59]

Jesus, the Light of the World

In the opening verses of John's Gospel we get a cosmic presentation of who Jesus is. Jesus is identified as the Logos, located in the

57. Hull, *In the Beginning*, 152–54.
58. Carson (*John*, 338) observes that "light" is a widespread religious symbol.
59. There is today also a discussion of metaphors of light and darkness in relation to race. See, e.g., the discussion in Olivia Gude, "Color Lines," *Learning for Justice* 19 (spring 2001), https://www.learningforjustice.org/magazine/spring-2001/color-lines.

beginning with God (John 1:1; cf. Gen. 1:1). "In him [the Logos], was life," John narrates, "and that life was the *light* of all humankind" (1:4). From here John introduces how light and darkness will play out through the Gospel, as "the light shines in the darkness, and the darkness has not overcome it" (1:5). Light goes on to represent revelation and salvation, while darkness connotes danger and evil.[60] In Jesus's dialogue with Nicodemus we learn that those who do evil avoid the light because they are in hiding; they don't want their deeds revealed. Those who live by the truth come into the light (3:19–21).

Jesus is called the "true light" (1:9), who came in the flesh. John says that no one has ever *seen* God, but God has been revealed to us because we have *seen* the glory of his one and only Son, full of grace and truth (1:14, 17–18). Jesus came to *reveal* God to the world, seeking to save those whom he loves, making them his children (1:12). And, once again, Jesus is set against the backdrop of Isaiah (42:6; 49:6), poised as the servant who is a *light* to the nations.[61]

Probably the most memorable light-related statement in John's Gospel is on Jesus's own lips when he claims, "I am the light of the world" (8:12). The setting of his words would have been highly significant. This is because it takes place during the Festival of Tabernacles, which was one of the most popular and joyous celebrations on the annual Jewish festal calendar. This festival commemorated the end of the annual harvest, and it recalled how God cared for Israel when he led them out of Egypt.[62] To celebrate, people from all over journeyed to Jerusalem and built temporary booths made from a variety of leafy branches, and they set up camp there for the week to celebrate. These booths reminded the Jews of how their ancestors lived in temporary shelters while wandering in the wilderness.

This weeklong festival involved several notable rituals, including a daily water ceremony (during which Jesus claims to provide living water [7:37–39]) and a nightly lamp-lighting ceremony. This one sounds pretty great. In the court of women at the temple were four huge candelabras, and young priests climbed ladders regularly to

60. John 1:4–5, 9–10; 3:19–21; 5:35; 8:12; 9:4–5; 11:9–10; 12:35–36, 46.
61. Keener, *John*, 1:739.
62. Lev. 23:33–36, 39–43; Deut. 16:13–15. For a more detailed portrayal, see Hanger, *Sensing Salvation*, chap. 3.

keep these lamps burning into the night while participants danced, sang, and celebrated. Keeping in mind the lack of electricity in those days, think about how this would transform the temple into a beautiful beacon of light. This was probably reminiscent of the pillar of fire that led Israel through the wilderness, night in and night out.[63] Significantly, this light also anticipated the messianic age.[64]

Now picture it: when Jesus states "I am the light of the world," it is during this weeklong festival, and he is standing in the temple treasury (8:20), right next to the court of women, where the nightly lamp-lighting took place. It would be hard not to be reminded of these sensory festivities—the singing, dancing, and especially the bright lights, along with their commemoration of God's lighted presence guiding Israel through the desert.

With this statement Jesus claims to be the light. But also, do you notice something familiar? In the previous chapter, we talked about Jesus making a similar claim ("I am the bread of life"). Something thematic is shaping up in John's Gospel: both statements begin with "I am" (in Greek, *egō eimi*), which for John and his readers links back to God's own identification (e.g., Deut. 32:39). Such a statement really riles things up with Jesus's audience, for it is understood to be a rather grand, potentially messianic claim.

Finally, notice how Jesus's statement in John 8:12 is accompanied by an invitation. Jesus invites anyone within earshot (including the readers of these words) to participate with him. "I am the light of the world," he says, and then adds, "Whoever follows me will never walk in darkness, but will have the light of life." Here I would suggest that "following" Jesus has salvific connotations: to follow him is what a disciple does. But *how* does one follow? The metaphor suggests the common notion of walking on a path to follow the light. Does this sound familiar? Just as the former generations of Israel threw a joyous party by giant lamplights to commemorate following the pillar of light through the desert, there is a sense in which "following Jesus" requires taking faith-filled steps in order to remain near Jesus, the light.

63. Exod. 13:21–22.
64. S. Brown, "Jesus in Word and Deed," 243–44, citing Exod. 13:21; Isa. 4:5.

Seeing the Embodied Light of the World

Within this salvific metaphor of staying near the light, it seems logical to suppose that one would need to *see* the light to do this. In the very next scene this "following the light of the world" metaphor is enacted when Jesus encounters a man who had been born blind. After resolving for the disciples that the man's visual deficit was unconnected to any sin (9:3), Jesus makes the "light" claim a second time: "While I am in the world, I am the light of the world" (9:5). Then, Jesus demonstrates *how* this is so by creating sight for—and thereby bringing light to—the man's eyes.[65] Do you notice the creation undertones in this gesture? Just as God formed a man from the dust of the ground (Gen. 2:7), Jesus uses the dust of the ground to create sight in the man's eyes as he "spit on the ground, made some mud with the saliva, and put it on the man's eyes" (9:6). After the man goes to wash in the Pool of Siloam, he comes back seeing (9:7).[66]

This is all the more Genesis-like when we consider that Jesus is not merely restoring sight that the man once knew but is creating an entirely new sensory ability for him. This is a rather sudden transformation, illustrating the eradicating effect light has on darkness. This man has never known sight before. Think of the social, economic, and religious effects of this sign. Since birth, this man has likely been shackled against his will to the common belief that his blindness was the result of his or his parents' sin (9:2).[67] His entire identity was shaped within a sighted culture. Note how he is narrated as begging (9:8); like Bartimaeus, this is probably one of his limited options for survival.

Here we can apply the same insights from our Synoptics discussion as we consider how Jesus used the humble sense of touch to create the more highly ranked sense of sight. His use of spit and dirt to anoint the man's eyes—and on the Sabbath, no less—contributes a hint of surprise and even controversy to the gesture.[68] Jesus, the

---

65. S. Brown, "Jesus in Word and Deed," 255–56.

66. S. Brown ("Jesus in Word and Deed," 255) notes also the emphasis that this gesture puts on Jesus providing life-giving water (7:37–38), as he uses the "living waters" of Siloam to create sight.

67. Cf. Gen. 25:22; Exod. 20:5.

68. See note 51 above, which highlights how spit could be perceived both negatively and positively.

preeminent light of the world, the Logos who was in the beginning with God, here draws close to the man with tactile familiarity. Recall how touch probably would be a significant way for this man to get along in his world. For Jesus to use touch to create sight perhaps would be a comforting way to engage with him.[69] Finally, consider how this is more than a one-sided gesture; it's an exchange. Jesus applies the mud paste, but the man does not see until he washes it away. This is an interactive miracle, one in which the man is invited to collaborate with "the light of the world."[70] It doesn't get more special than this.

Jesus's gesture has a profound effect on both the man and his community. John narrates the struggle that it is for others to come to terms with his newly sighted presence. His neighbors barely recognize him (9:8–11): *Isn't this the guy who used to sit and beg?* The Pharisees are dumbfounded. One of the obstacles is that Jesus performs this sign on the Sabbath, which for them is a marker that he can't be doing God's work (9:16, 29). And yet giving sight to the blind has messianic and divine implications, which they seem very reluctant to apply to Jesus. Eager to get to the bottom of things, they put the witnesses on trial. First up: the man's parents, who buckle in fear. In their testimony they defer to their son: *Ask him. He's an adult. He can answer for himself* (9:20–23). The formerly blind man is the one person who *knows* what happened. Throughout the scene he testifies by falling repeatedly back on his encounter with Jesus (9:11, 15, 25, 30): *I don't know what more to tell y'all. He made some mud, put it on my eyes, told me to go wash, so I did. I was blind, but now I see!* The man himself makes progress in his understanding of who Jesus is. He goes from only knowing Jesus's name (9:11), to supposing Jesus is a prophet (9:17), to suggesting Jesus *must* be from God (9:32–33), to finally declaring belief. At this point he truly "sees" who Jesus is and worships him as the Son of Man (9:35–38).

The Gospel of John was the first biblical book that John Hull read in braille after losing his sight completely. He recounts how this once-cherished text created unease when he read anew the

69. Hanger, *Sensing Salvation*, 81.
70. Hanger, *Sensing Salvation*, 82.

blindness-unbelief, sight-faith parallels of John 9. It's so "absolute," he writes, "either you are blind or you are sighted, in light or in darkness."[71] Jaime Clark-Soles observes that when Jesus meets up with the Pharisees in the final scene and declares them blind (9:39), this, alas, "is a code word for 'ignorant.'"[72] Clark-Soles continues, "Jesus, the light, has come into the world and is shining in the faces of the religious leaders. They hate the light and want to do the evil deed of disabling Jesus through death. The man born blind sees the light and does the work of God by believing in Jesus."[73] This is where the metaphor gets flipped, as Hull points out that there is the same disconnect between blindness and sin reflected in Jesus's initial declaration that the man's blindness was not the result of sin: "Sin lies in the self-deception of those who believe that they have insight but do not."[74] In the case of these Pharisees, they are physically sighted and claim to "see," but they "claim too much for themselves with respect to insight, and commit the sin of willful ignorance."[75]

Despite the negative correlations between blindness and unbelief and between sight and faith, one thing to keep in mind is how this man with a visual impairment is an exemplary character in John, someone we are all called to emulate.[76] Moreover, his ability to see Jesus, the light of the world, was tied to his receptivity to Jesus's touch. Jesus engaged him in a dialogue that transformed his life and gave him the resource to follow on the path to stay near the light.

Sight for the Earliest Readers

Once again, the earliest ancient readers of these Gospel narratives would have "seen" more than the characters within the narratives do. Readers and rereaders of these stories pick up on the wider themes of sight that materialize across each Gospel as a whole. Along with this, remember that all readers approach Jesus's words

71. Hull, *In the Beginning*, 87.
72. Clark-Soles, *Reading John*, 55.
73. Clark-Soles, *Reading John*, 55.
74. Hull, *In the Beginning*, 50.
75. Clark-Soles, *Reading John*, 56.
76. Clark-Soles, *Reading John*, 47.

retrospectively, understanding these various scenes from a postresurrection viewpoint.

This means that the way the Synoptic Gospels present Jesus in the Isaianic stream as a light for the nations would have given ancient readers a sense of connection between the words of the prophets, the words of John the Baptizer, and the works of Jesus in the Gospels in fulfillment of this messianic vocation, which includes bringing sight to the blind. Moreover, anywhere we see the temple make an appearance in the Gospels, it can be fruitful to consider how post–AD 70 ancient readers might have interacted with these scenes, such as with Jesus's claim to be the light of the world during the Festival of Tabernacles. If the temple no longer stood as they read, would there have been nostalgia and a sense of loss for those who were within living memory of the lamp-lighting ceremony? Would Jesus's words "I am the light" have been received as a comfort?

I suspect that ancient readers would have had a better pulse on the implications for those whom Jesus healed of their visual impairments. This would have played out in social, economic, and religious ways as newly sighted people would have been able to participate in their communities in ways they hadn't before. I wonder also how Jesus's compassion for those on the margins would have proliferated into the ancient church ethos, supplying resource for those with all kinds of needs.

Reflections on Sight for Modern Readers

Blessings for Those Who Have Not Seen

Perhaps an appropriate way to think about sight for modern and the earliest readers is by looking at one of the final postresurrection scenes in John. In one of the earliest appearances of Jesus to his disciples (John 20:19–23), we learn that Thomas was not there; he missed it completely. When the other disciples report to him, "We have seen the Lord!" (20:25a), his response comes off as rather cynical, earning him the moniker "doubting Thomas."[77] He says something

---

77. While it's common to interpret this scene as Thomas's struggle with doubt, some commentators point out that if he carries through on his declaration, "I will never believe!" (20:25b), this will effectively leave him in a state of persistent unbelief. See,

to the effect of, *If I can't see Jesus for myself, I'll never believe!*[78] Can we blame him? I'd be disappointed too, if I were in his position. But wait: I *am* in his position. You are too. We *haven't* seen the resurrected Jesus in the flesh. And all of us must decide whether we will believe despite our lack of sight.

What's really going on here is that Thomas is unwilling to believe the testimony of his own friends who *have* seen Jesus in the flesh. When he finally gets to see Jesus for himself, he declares belief: "My Lord and my God!" (20:28). And here Thomas's desire to *see* Jesus connects to us as readers, because Jesus says to Thomas, "Because you have *seen* me, you have believed; blessed are those who have *not seen* and yet have believed" (20:29). That's us! Every believer who has not seen Jesus in the flesh relies on the testimony of this first generation of disciples who *have* seen him. And Jesus declares us blessed as we live out this faith.[79]

How Seeing and Not Seeing Bolster Faith

As we have discussed throughout this chapter, sighted people are prone to engage their eyes "automatically," without giving much thought to this action. It is not until we consider lack of sight that we offer it the reflection it deserves, and so I appreciate and agree with Hull's comment that "without blind people, the religious experience of sighted people is not complete."[80] Because of the tendency to take sight for granted, seeing might be the easiest sense to become overly reliant on. Depending on sight more than we should can get us into trouble, such as encouraging our propensity to judge by appearances. Overreliance on sight can go so far as to impede faith. Hebrews 11:1 reminds us, "Faith is the assurance of things hoped for, the conviction of things *not* seen" (NRSVue), and 2 Corinthians

---

for example, Thompson, *John*, 425. Klink (*John*, 878) suggests that this is not so much doubt as potential rebellion. He adds that here Thomas wants to believe, but "only on his terms."

78. This may sound more emphatic than you might read in some English translations. The NIV simply says, "I will not believe," but the construction in the Greek has the literal sense of "I will never believe" (as in the ESV).

79. Thompson, *John*, 377.

80. Hull, *In the Beginning*, 132.

5:7 is similar: "We walk by faith, *not* by sight" (NRSVue).[81] These Scriptures demonstrate how it is the *absence* of sight that defines faith.

Hull raises the honest and captivating question, Why doesn't God simply restore everyone's sight? *Yeah, why doesn't he?* I find myself wondering. The answer is simple, but it gut-punched me when I read it: "Then God would not have to guide us."[82] All of this retraces a theme we encountered in the previous chapter, which is that perhaps dependence on Someone Else is not a bad thing but is actually the goal. Hull punctuates these thoughts with words from the third Servant Song (Isa. 50:4–11), which upholds blind people as the model: "Who among you fears the LORD and obeys the word of his servant? Let the one who walks in the dark, who has no light, trust in the name of the LORD and rely on their God" (50:10). What a picture! What a worthy goal: to be like the servant who can walk through darkness with "calm assurance," trusting in the Lord with confidence.[83]

There is much to celebrate about the sensory faculty of sight. It is a good gift from the Lord to be able to see, and our eyes can enlighten us about God's magnificent world. The Gospels reminds us that the coming of the kingdom of God is marked by Jesus restoring sight to those who are blind. However, if we think of these miracles only in physical terms, we miss the abundance of what's going on. Hull reminds us that these miracles are always set within the context of enacting justice and alleviating oppression.[84] In God's economy and within the sensory conversation, to be sighted is not necessarily the highest good. Rather, the highest good is for the sighted *and* the nonsighted to be included, to be accepted, and to be restored to community (Jer. 31:8; Mic. 4:5–6).[85] Going forward, as we consider the role of sight in engaging Jesus with our senses, may we continue to seek ways to deepen our faith and dependence on him.

81. Hull, *In the Beginning*, 142.
82. Hull, *In the Beginning*, 111. He goes on, "It looks as if God likes us the way we are."
83. Hull, *In the Beginning*, 111–12.
84. Hull, *In the Beginning*, 113.
85. Hull, *In the Beginning*, 112.

INSIGHTS
TO LIGHT THE PATH

1. Jesus is associated with light in the Fourth Gospel narrative. This exercise is designed to take about an hour but can be extended. Start by spending fifteen minutes reflecting on John 8, remembering what we discussed about the Festival of Tabernacles setting when Jesus states, "I am the light of the world." Next, spend another fifteen minutes in complete darkness. (Please ensure you are in a safe location in whatever setting you decide to do this.) During this time, ask God to continue to reveal himself to you. Now, introduce a gentle light into view, whether it's a candle, a small lamp, or a flashlight. For another fifteen minutes reflect on how God led Israel through the desert by light. Consider how Jesus the light invites you to follow him. For the final fifteen minutes, journal your thoughts. Reflect on the following:

   a. What new insights did you come away with?

   b. How has this impacted your own posture toward Jesus as the light of the world?

2. What is it like not to have sight? For this exercise, partner up with someone with whom you can share this experience. Take turns experimenting with what it's like to navigate the world without sight. For this exercise, take a walk with your friend. For one half of the walk, have one person cover their eyes while the other one leads them along the path. Then, reverse these roles. Here are some questions to take with you on your journey:

   a. What is it like to lead or be led when one of you cannot see?

   b. Pay attention to what you are hearing, smelling, and feeling as you are led. What do you notice afresh when you are without sight?

   c. Finally, how might this experience correlate to your reflections on walking by faith?

5

Hearing the Divine Call

Jesus Who Speaks
and the Sheep That Follow

Sounds are powerful. They burrow deep into our minds, our bodies, our memories, and our emotions. Frederick Douglass affirms the potency of sound in his 1855 autobiographical reflection on his life both as a slave and after his emancipation, where he reminisces about frequent singing among fellow slaves. He corrects the common appraisal of slaves as "happy laborers," commenting, "It is a great mistake to suppose them happy because they sing."[1] In the first place, he says that slaves often were made to sing by their owners and overseers as a way of tracking where they were.[2] Amid all their singing—whether obligatory or freely engaged—he remembers the rich tones of complaint, anguish, and sadness. Singing was an exercise of reversal, attempting to relieve the heart when it was stripped of hope, a straining toward respite, seeking to create happiness rather than express it.[3] He

1. Douglass, *My Bondage*, 99.
2. Douglass, *My Bondage*, 97.
3. Douglass, *My Bondage*, 100.

specifically reminisces about the sounds of monthly allowance day at Colonel Lloyd's plantation, when slaves would travel to collect their rations of food. He recalls the "wild notes," boisterous but not happy, with a "tinge of deep melancholy."[4] He talks both about the potency of these sounds and about the *effect* that the mere remembering of this scene has on him:

> I have sometimes thought, that the mere hearing of those songs would do more to impress truly spiritual-minded men and women with the soul-crushing and death-dealing character of slavery, than the reading of whole volumes of its mere physical cruelties. They speak to the heart and to the soul of the thoughtful. . . . Every tone was a testimony against slavery, and a prayer to God for deliverance from chains. . . . The mere recurrence, even now, afflicts my spirit, and while I am writing these lines, my tears are falling. To those songs I trace my first glimmering conceptions of the dehumanizing character of slavery.[5]

For Douglass, these songs carried a haunting effect; he couldn't get away from them. They served to heighten his hatred of slavery while strengthening his compassion for those still enslaved.[6]

As we explore the sense of hearing, let's continue to imagine together the richness of our lives as sensory beings. Douglass impresses on us how hearing sound can make indelible marks on our minds, our bodies, our hearts, and our actions. Can you relate to this experience, where a sound reverberates loudly in your soul because of the associative memory it carries? It can be as simple as listening to an old favorite song or even an old *least* favorite song. Notice how feelings of either nostalgia or dismay said song will dredge up within. Many times, like in Douglass's case, remembered sounds can move us to action.

In our shift from considering sight to exploring sound in the biblical text, we are going to encounter some similar dynamics alongside some new ones. For example, comparable to how the sight of

4. Douglass, *My Bondage*, 98.
5. Douglass, *My Bondage*, 98–99.
6. Douglass, *My Bondage*, 99.

Jesus—the light of the world—invites us to use our eyes, Jesus's *voice* carries weight, and we are invited to respond through our sense of hearing: *Whoever has ears to hear, let them hear.* As in the previous chapter, we will confront negative portrayals of those who lack a sensory ability like hearing. We will explore how Jesus restores hearing and speech to many people throughout the Gospels. And we will also consider the effect of the divine voice for those within earshot. Before we do, however, let's inspect the character of hearing and its role in modern and ancient contexts.

Exploring Hearing

From the outset let me suggest that in our modern, Western, tech-savvy context, hearing has a lot in common with sight in terms of how much we rely on it for day-to-day life. For those who live in largely urban and even suburban contexts, you might find that you have to travel a long way out of town before you can find silence. However, even when we *can* find silent physical spaces, it doesn't mean true silence, as we are often prone to fill these spaces with noise. In fact, for many of us, I'm guessing that silence feels foreign. Something feels missing if there is not music or the hum of a TV in the background, or if there are not listening devices plugged into our ears. We are so accustomed to noise that we even buy "white noise" machines to fall asleep to. Sound can be such a comfort. Most of the time.

There are times, however, when sound interferes with our peace. Words on a page or a screen can create proverbial "noise" in our minds, displaying a common partnership between sight and sound. Our eyes and ears ingest content, which fills our minds so that we are constantly brimming over with information, and reels, and to-do lists, and problems, and solutions. This is an inner type of "noise" that enters our physically silent spaces. This is noise that invades the quiet of our hearts, our sense of tranquility. All of this brings up a series of questions surrounding the effects of noise in our lives: In what ways does noise create anxiety? In what ways does it create comfort? How should we relate to sound? Some are constantly asking how to find silence. Others are asking, Why would we want to?

The Anatomy of Hearing

Hearing is similar to the anatomy of sight in that it too is experienced in a more distanced fashion. Sound is carried across the air, reaching the ear in a more passive manner than some of the more intimate and direct perceptions like taste or touch.[7] The ear has been described as being more vulnerable than other receptors that have covers, like eyelids for eyes, and lips for a tongue. The ear, by contrast, is always vulnerable to sound and is without defense. It is "unreflectively accumulative, naively open to even the most harmful of loud, high, concussive sounds."[8]

One of the aspects of hearing that we must address is its close connection to the presence of speech in the Gospels. On the one hand, we could make a good argument that speech is its own physical sense, separate from hearing.[9] But on the other hand, there is a good case to be made for considering speech and hearing together, since in many places they are inseparable, such as when sheep *hear* the *voice* of the shepherd calling them by name (John 10:1–18).[10] For this reason, this chapter on hearing will include speech in the conversation, and I will point out where speech plays a significant role.

Hearing in Modern and Ancient Contexts

In the previous chapter we talked about life in a sight-centric world, both today and in an ancient context. In chapter 1 we discussed how

---

7. Aristotle, *On the Soul* 2.420a5.

8. Bull and Back, *Auditory Culture Reader*, 487.

9. I actually have made a case to understand speech as a separate sense (Hanger, *Sensing Salvation*, 88–89). There I discuss how we don't often conceive of speech as its own physical sense because we tend to think of the senses as passive in operation. Noises and fragrances are external data we perceive as they enter our sphere. By contrast, speech is something we engage actively. Also, since speech is an acquired ability—it's something we learn—then it doesn't really fit in with "natural" operations like the five senses. So a case can be made for speech as its own physical sense, separate from hearing. Speaking requires that we use breath to make noise through our mouths, while hearing is received passively through our ears. Avrahami (*Senses of Scripture*) also treats these as separate sense perceptions. See also Classen, *Worlds of Sense*, 2.

10. Avrahami (*Senses of Scripture*, 109) talks about there being such a strong link between hearing and speech that they often are considered to be aspects of one sense.

Aristotle considered sight to be at the top of the hierarchy of senses. Because of this, sight tends to get all the attention. However, hearing is not far behind: Aristotle ranked hearing right up there at the top, just below sight. This helps to explain why hearing in our world is also often equated with philosophy, symbolically employed to denote understanding.[11] These connections are what preserve sight and hearing as "higher" forms of reasoning, while smell, taste, and touch are considered more inferior, "animal," and "servile."[12]

In Scripture, as in our world, hearing sits alongside sight as a common way of talking about faith or understanding. The most prominent example in the Gospels is Jesus's recurring refrain mentioned above: "Whoever has ears to hear, let them hear" (e.g., Matt. 11:15; Mark 4:9; Luke 8:8). Notice how this statement is about more than physical hearing: it indicates a kind of understanding leading to transformation, response, and action. John's Jesus similarly states, "Whoever hears my word and believes him who sent me has eternal life" (John 5:24).

Now, there has been important conversation through the years about how some non-Western, less literate cultures were more aural (focused on hearing) than visual. Back in the 1960s, two communication scholars, Marshall McLuhan and Walter Ong, conducted important work in this area, suggesting that a culture's tendency to privilege one sense over all others was directly related to technological innovations that fostered the elevation of that sense.[13] Using the example of sight in the modern West, we see a correlation between the high rank of sight and the development and reliance on the printing press, reading and writing, the telescope and microscope, and so forth. These visual activities have contributed to more distanced ways of relating to the world, which also fueled the development of abstract thought.

This led McLuhan and Ong to suggest a division of the human world into literate/visual and aural/oral cultures. This dichotomy

---

11. Avrahami, *Senses of Scripture*, 158.

12. Philo, *On Abraham* 29.149. Korsmeyer (*Making Sense of Taste*, 3) observes how taste, touch, and smell are considered the more "bodily" and therefore "lower" senses.

13. This discussion is based on background provided by Avrahami, *Senses of Scripture*, 8–10.

ultimately was criticized for its lack of nuance; not all cultures fit cleanly into one box or another.[14] Our study here is not about trying to parse all of this out. But McLuhan and Ong's work does highlight how Western scholars prioritize sight. And for our purposes it will be helpful to understand how the ancient world probably was more aural/oral than what we experience today in modern, urban/suburban, Western contexts. In other words, hearing, while ranked below sight, likely played a prominent role in the ancient world.

Life in a society before the invention of the printing press would have been different.[15] Words on a first-century page were not mass produced; they were transcribed by a small subset of people—scribes—skilled in writing and copying texts. This means that the general population probably learned in part by hearing. While we often speak about the earliest "readers" of the Gospels, most ancient communities would have first encountered the Gospels as "listeners."[16] The Gospel stories themselves would have first circulated orally, publicly, even dramatically.[17] Even after they were written down by scribes, these texts would generally have been read in public (as opposed to in private), as literacy rates were lower among the earliest Christians than what we tend to see today. Now, from here we could diverge down a fascinating rabbit trail into questions about what the Gospels—in their earliest performances—looked *and* sounded like, and even what they smelled like. There is a vast set of multisensory possibilities wrapped up in the earliest iterations of the stories about Jesus's life and words. Of course, we will stay on track, but all of this reminds us that our own (mostly visual) encounters with the Gospels as texts may be different from how the earliest communities received them.

These dynamics also apply to the narrative world of the Gospel stories themselves, set as they are in the first century. It makes sense of

14. Avrahami (*Senses of Scripture*, 22–31) talks about the debate around the character of biblical thought and the problematic ways that the "Hebrew," or "primitive (or worse, 'savage') mind" formed a dichotomy against "modern thought," which corresponds to other distinctions like Western/Eastern or Greek/Hebrew thought.

15. Johannes Gutenberg invented the movable type printing press in 1440 in Germany.

16. Lawrence, *Sense and Stigma*, 21; Sandy, *Hear Ye the Word of the Lord*.

17. Performance criticism is a discipline that examines how the earliest texts within an oral/scribal culture would have been transmitted by way of a performance event.

Jesus as an itinerant teacher in public spaces, interpreting texts that crowds would have little access to compared with the spiritual leaders of their day. A high premium, therefore, would be placed on being able to hear and to speak since this would be a prominent method for communicating important truths to wide swaths of people. Hearing and speaking are, of course, still an important mode of communication in the modern world. But we engage these media differently today than they did back then.

Hearing and Deafness in Scripture

As we prepare to explore the text, I want to draw on the previous chapter's introduction of sensory disabilities,[18] since much of that will apply here. Alongside those who lacked sight, those who were deaf and/or mute likewise would have been cast to the margins of society. Some of this was due to an inability to earn a living and participate in day-to-day life without considerable difficulty. That the Scriptures call for justice for these groups is evidence that they were in fact recipients of injustice (Lev. 19:14). This contributes to the perception that those with sensory disabilities were helpless, and this in turn correlates with prejudices applied to those with sensory disabilities, such as supposing that these persons must be under divine judgment related to their sin.[19]

We will soon explore how Jesus brings hearing and speech to several people in the various Gospel accounts (e.g., Mark 7:37). Similar to Jesus bringing sight to the blind, these kinds of healings speak to his messianic vocation, confirmed for John the Baptizer when he sends messengers to ask if Jesus is "the one who is to come." Jesus replies, "Go back and report to John what you hear and see: The blind receive sight, the lame walk, those who have leprosy are cleansed, the deaf hear, the dead are raised, and the good news is proclaimed to the poor" (Matt. 11:4–5; cf. Luke 7:22). As we've observed, Jesus's arrival ushers in the kingdom of God, in line with the Isaianic voice whereby "the eyes of the blind will be opened and the ears of the deaf unstopped" (Isa. 35:5). Let's turn now to address

18. See "Sight and Blindness in Scripture" in chap. 4.
19. Avrahami, *Senses of Scripture*, 207–8.

specific instances of hearing alongside prominent voices speaking in the Synoptic accounts.

Hearing in the Synoptics

Scholars who study the senses in the Scriptures are quick to point out the overlap and even the inextricable collaboration of the senses with one another. Brittany Wilson talks about how Luke-Acts presents seeing and hearing as working together in complementary fashion as they depict "the extra-ordinary experience of encountering the divine."[20] She critiques readings of the text that elevate hearing to the top of a sensory hierarchy as a way of prioritizing the divine word. She points out that since sight is so often linked to knowledge and understanding, it quite often functions right alongside divine speech as a way of making sense of human encounters with the divine. She ultimately concludes that for Luke-Acts, "hearing and seeing are the most important in accounts of divine-human encounters."[21] As we delve into a study of hearing in the Synoptics, let's begin with our first significant example of this synaesthetic dynamic. It involves two scenes that appear in all three Synoptic Gospels.

The Voice from Heaven

In the early scenes of Matthew, Mark, and Luke we read about how Jesus is baptized in the Jordan River by John. All three Gospels report that immediately after Jesus emerges from the water, the heavens open—Mark more vividly says the heavens are "torn" open—and the Spirit of God descends on Jesus in bodily form like a dove. And then, a voice comes from heaven, saying, "You are my Son, whom I love; with you I am well pleased" (Matt. 3:16–17; Mark 1:10–11; Luke 3:21–22).

We could spend pages dissecting each Gospel's setting and word choice in order to understand their particular emphases.[22] For our

20. Wilson, "Seeing Divine Speech," 253.
21. Wilson, "Seeing Divine Speech," 269.
22. For example, Matthew alone mentions that Jesus saw the Spirit descending, and the divine voice appears to be framed in a more public manner, in the third

purposes, let's focus on the visual and auditory quality of this heavenly revelation. First things first: this scene gives off familiar apocalyptic vibes; the opening of the heavens is a common way of talking about divine revelation.[23] In this heavenly vision the divine voice "confirms and interprets" the descending Spirit,[24] saying, "You are my Son, whom I love."

Some have suggested that this scene presents God as "breaking his silence" after so many years; he is now speaking through his Son,[25] commissioning Jesus's ministry as it gets underway. The Spirit descending on Jesus and the divine voice together convey God's affirmation of Jesus's sonship.[26] Notice in all of this how sight and hearing work in concert with each other.

You probably won't be surprised to learn that the divine words are reminiscent of several significant Old Testament texts. One of the most commonly cited connections presents Jesus once again in line with the suffering servant: "Here is my servant, whom I uphold, my chosen one in whom I delight; I will put my Spirit on him, and he will bring justice to the nations" (Isa. 42:1). At the same time, these words may combine with the royal imagery of Psalm 2:7, in which the Lord speaks of the royal king he has installed on Zion: "He said to me, 'You are my son; today I have become your father.'" Finally, some see this affirmation of sonship as hearkening back to Abraham's son Isaac in Genesis 22:2, when God directs Abraham to "take your son, your only son whom you love" and offer him up as a sacrifice.[27]

In the wake of this baptism the Spirit of God has descended to rest on Jesus. This empowering presence, combined with the divine voice of approval, lends authentication to Jesus as the beloved Son

---

person, "This is my Son," rather than the second person in Mark and Luke, "You are my Son."

23. For example, Ezek. 1:1, 25; Acts 7:56; Rev. 4:1. See Green, *Luke*, 185; Turner, *Matthew*, 119–20.

24. Turner, *Matthew*, 120.

25. Turner, *Matthew*, 120.

26. Green (*Luke*, 185) understands Luke's emphasis to be less on the baptism and more on God bestowing the Spirit on Jesus along with his affirmation of sonship.

27. Beavis (*Mark*, 36) acknowledges the difficulty in pinpointing just one text, citing Matera ("Key to Mark's Gospel," 18n31), who suggests that the evangelist expects readers to notice all three allusions.

of God and establishes him on his earthly trajectory. From here he sets out into his divinely ordained ministry with authority on earth to accomplish his mission.

This is not the only time that Jesus is affirmed with such audiovisual majesty. Later in his ministry—also represented in every Synoptic account—Jesus takes his closest friends up to a mountaintop where they experience a grand heavenly vision of Christ (Matt. 17:1–9; Mark 9:2–10; Luke 9:28–36). Here, Mark can't seem to find an adequate earthly equivalent to capture Jesus's transformation into magnificent glory. The best he can do is describe Jesus's clothes as "whiter than anyone in the world could bleach them" (9:3). Many detect hints of Moses's radiant face following his encounter with the Lord on Mount Sinai (Exod. 34:29–35),[28] and this combines with the mountain setting, a common "meeting-place between human beings and God, between the temporal and the eternal, between past, present, and future."[29] This scene seems to be a cross between an apocalyptic vision of the kingdom of God and an epiphany (where a heavenly being appears to humanity with a message, like when Gabriel appeared to Mary).[30]

Out of this "bright cloud" comes a voice that once again bestows divine pleasure. God says, "This is my Son, whom I love; with him I am well pleased. Listen to him!" (Matt. 17:5).[31] Some have suggested that the divine voice is the climactic point of the encounter, and we might think so based on Matthew's comment that it was the *hearing* of this voice that laid the disciples out, prostrate in fear (17:6). However, sight and hearing are once again working together. The visual transfiguration of Jesus reveals his true heavenly colors, and now the audible voice comes in to complete the vision, to explain it.[32]

---

28. Beavis, *Mark*, 135–36.

29. Lee, *Transfiguration*, 2.

30. Lee (*Transfiguration*, 5) views the transfiguration as a complementary mix of these two genres—apocalyptic vision and epiphany—"depict[ing] Jesus as he will be at his future coming, a coming already anticipated in his ministry and resurrection." Heil (*Matthew*, 82) also understands this as a glimpse into Jesus's "future coming in heavenly glory," and Beavis (*Mark*, 135) understands this as foreshadowing the "glorious eschatological manifestation of the son of man."

31. Only in Matthew does the voice say, "With him I am well pleased." Luke: "This is my Son, whom I have chosen" (9:35); Mark: "This is my Son, whom I love" (9:7).

32. Lee, *Transfiguration*, 23.

Notice how such interpretation is necessary, as Peter doesn't quite understand what's happening. He initially tries to figure out a way to set up camp and linger in this special moment. The voice is "an unimpeachable source" identifying who Jesus is along with his mission. This then forms the basis for the instruction to "listen" to him.[33]

The disciples have been given insight into who Jesus truly is. It's easy to focus on the disciples' response of facedown fear and forget that Peter's first words to Jesus were, "Lord, it is good for us to be here" (Mark 9:5). *Can we stay awhile?* The disciples are overwhelmed by the sight of this encounter, but in the best way possible. Dorothy Lee names what they witness: it's the beauty of Christ, "a beauty associated with light and glory, and confirmed in the speech of the divine voice."[34] With this encounter comes a sense of hope; this vision provides the kind of "joyful expectation" that will fuel the disciples' own future "proclamation of the good news."[35]

Let's keep moving through the Synoptics and follow the through line of the divine voice. The divine voice from heaven has exhorted Jesus's followers to listen to Jesus. As we turn to Jesus's own voice, let's examine who hears it, and let's contemplate its weight.

The Voice of Jesus

The first thing to notice about Jesus's voice is that it carries the kind of authority that commands attention, particularly over oppressive demonic powers. Matthew reports an evening occasion when Jesus was healing the sick and helping the demon-possessed, stating that he "drove out the spirits with a *word*" (Matt. 8:16). Sometimes these spirits terrorized people by casting them into silence; those in bondage are described as being mute. When Jesus drives out one such demon from a man who could not speak, the man's voice is immediately restored (Matt. 9:32–33; cf. Luke 11:14). Finally, just as Jesus drives out demons and restores men and women from their own silence, his voice carries the authority to silence the voices of

33. Green, *Luke*, 384. This may allude to the promised "prophet like Moses" (Deut. 18:15) (377).
34. Lee, *Transfiguration*, 128.
35. Lee, *Transfiguration*, 124.

these very same spiritual oppressors. Luke reports that many spirits, upon being driven away by Jesus, shout, "You are the Son of God!" and Jesus rebukes them into silence, his voice disallowing them from speaking (Luke 4:41).

Jesus's voice is described as carrying authority over nature. The most prominent example of this is when Jesus calms a storm. All three Synoptic Gospel writers report this event, once again with differing emphases. It's interesting that the sense of hearing is never mentioned outright, but in three-part harmony we can read how Jesus's voice is the catalyst for the storm to subside: "Jesus rebuked the wind and the raging waters" (Luke 8:24; cf. Matt. 8:26; Mark 4:39). Mark says that Jesus rebuked the wind and actually said *to the waves*, "Quiet! Be still!" This has an immediate effect: "Then the wind died down and it was completely calm" (Mark 4:39). This freaks the disciples out in the best way possible because they see the correlation between Jesus's voice and the calming of the tempest. The turn of events is narrated as so immediate that one might think that hearing is mentioned. It's not, but surely it must be implied. Nature "hears" Jesus's voice and submits to it.

The calming of the storm is reminiscent of the kind of authority that God is described as having in the Old Testament, such as in the parting of the sea during the exodus (Exod. 14:21–31). The Psalms often present God as having power over the waves, such as when the psalmist states, "He stilled the storm to a whisper; the waves of the sea were hushed" (Ps. 107:29).[36] Finally, have you ever thought about how this scene connects with the story of Jonah? Jonah, of course, is running away from God when he boards a boat heading to Tarshish. A storm kicks up while Jonah—like Jesus—is asleep in the boat. It is only after the sailors wake Jonah up and throw him overboard that the storm finally ceases. This obviously is not exactly the same way that Jesus calms the storm! These parallels convey that someone greater than Jonah has arrived.[37] But note in Jonah's story how the stilled sea prompts a fear of God among the sailors rivaling the fear of the

---

36. Cf. Pss. 42:7–8; 65:7–8; 89:8–9. See Beavis, *Mark*, 91–92. Note especially Ps. 107, which connects rather well to Mark's version of the story.

37. Strauss, *Mark*, 206.

disciples after they witness Jesus's authority over the waves: "Who is this? Even the wind and waves obey him!" (Mark 4:41).[38]

Jesus's voice has authority over life and death. In Luke's Gospel, we read about a time when Jesus's compassion stops a funeral procession to raise the only son of a widow as he is being carried out on a bier (7:11–17). Jesus simply says, "Young man, I say to you, get up!" The response is immediate: "The dead man sat up and began to talk" (7:15). Once again, hearing is implied. How does this "dead man" respond to Jesus's voice if he's not hearing it? This scene is frequently viewed alongside that of Elijah raising the widow's son because of several significant parallels (1 Kings 17:17–24). The similarities also serve to highlight the contrasts. One common observation is the difference between how Elijah expends a lot of energy praying and pleading with God on behalf of the woman and her son, whereas Jesus simply speaks directly to the dead body. Joel Green calls this a "speech-act" that is evidence of Jesus's authority, status, and role in God's saving purposes.[39]

Therefore, Jesus's voice carries weight through the Synoptics. He is able to silence spirits in the demonic realm and by doing so to release the tongues of those who had been under oppression. His voice speaks into the chaos of the natural world and brings peace. And finally, Jesus's voice carries the authority to call life out of death.

True Hearing

Earlier in this chapter we mentioned Jesus's common refrain and invitation, "Whoever has ears to hear, let them hear." This is famously placed at the end of the parable of the sower (a title that is somewhat of a misnomer because the parable focuses more on the soils) (Matt. 13:1–9; Mark 4:1–9; Luke 8:4–8). Here Jesus compares people to the quality of soil they represent when the seeds of the word are sown into their lives. Do you resemble the soil along the path, which is

---

38. Beavis (*Mark*, 92) describes an influential interpretation of this passage that reads this miracle as a kind of exorcism. Jesus rebukes the chaotic waters much like he rebukes the demonic forces. This story sets up the stories of exorcism in Mark to follow.

39. Green, *Luke*, 292.

vulnerable to birds that snatch the seeds away before they can sprout? Is your soil rocky and more likely to stunt the growth of the seeds? Is it thorny and thus inhospitable to good, deep roots? The ideal soil, the "good" soil, allows for deep roots and lush growth. This, Jesus says, is like the person who has "ears to hear" and is receptive to the word as it takes root and produces a crop.

This is very similar to another example Jesus gives, where "hearing" must result in action. Jesus says that those who hear his words and put them into practice are like the man who builds his house on a foundation of rock, which will withstand a storm. Those who hear his words but do *not* put them into practice are like one who does not build on a strong foundation; their house will crumble in a storm (Matt. 7:21–27; Luke 6:46–49). This is similar to Jesus's comment about who his true family is: "My mother and brothers are those who *hear* God's word and put it into practice" (Luke 8:21). True hearing must lead to action.

Thus, Jesus warns potential disciples, "Consider carefully how you listen" (Luke 8:18). In this way hearing is closely allied with faith. It involves both the ears and the heart; it's about receptivity. Most importantly, this is a type of hearing related to Jesus's own voice. Like the storm and the dead man, will those who listen to Jesus's voice really hear it? Will they respond favorably in receptivity and faith?

In this final section let's address places in the Synoptic narratives where Jesus restores hearing. Similar to how we experienced the man born blind being given sight to see the light of the world (John 9), we will witness the messianic vocation being articulated through the restoration of hearing, so that disciples may hear the voice of Jesus.

Jesus Heals Those Who Are Deaf and Mute

In her 2011 sensory survey of the Gospel of Mark, New Testament scholar Louise Lawrence reports that Mark is an audio-centric text. In Mark's world, someone doesn't have to see in order to believe. Instead, hearing and speech are considered essential. Sight is "statistically important," but the Greek word for "hear" (*akouō*) occurs around forty times in Mark. She concludes that ultimately "the gravest sensory impairment within Mark's world is to be deaf and without speech."[40] In the following we will explore two such Markan examples.

Directly following the transfiguration, Jesus encounters a man whose son is possessed by a spirit (Mark 9:14–29). This spirit has "robbed" him of speech (9:17),[41] and it has been throwing him into violent seizures since he was a kid. Jesus addresses this "deaf and mute spirit" directly, commanding it to leave the boy for good.[42] The spirit doesn't come out without a convulsive fight, but ultimately the boy is healed. Note here not only that Jesus restores the boy's hearing and speech but also that it's the sound of Jesus's voice that is the impetus for the spirit to leave and that ultimately restores the boy to health.

The second scene we will explore is unique to Mark (7:31–37). It takes place in the Decapolis, in gentile territory. Several people bring to Jesus a man who is deaf and struggles to speak. Note the similarities to Jesus's encounter with the blind man at Bethsaida: Jesus pulls the man away from the crowd in order to address him, and he heals by touching his affected organs—in this case, his ears and tongue. Jesus puts his fingers in the man's ears, and he uses his spit as he touches the man's tongue. He looks up to heaven (probably prayerfully), sighs deeply, and says, "Be opened!" Some have associated Jesus's distinct actions with formulas employed by miracle workers.[43] This entire tactile, vocal gesture conveys a unique quality of compassion.[44]

With Isaiah 35:5–6 in the background, the man's ears "were opened," and his tongue was "loosened" so that he could speak clearly.[45] This scene may also recall the concern that Moses expresses to God that he

40. Lawrence, "Exploring the Sense-scape," 392–93.
41. Lawrence's claim that Mark is audio-centric bears up when you look at his account alongside Matthew (17:14–21) and Luke (9:37–43a). The latter two present the boy as struggling with seizures, with no mention of the spirit denying him speech or hearing.
42. Strauss (Mark, 399) points out that the spirit itself is not mute and deaf but is instead preventing the boy from speaking and hearing. He prefers the NRSV, in which Jesus says, "You spirit that keeps this boy from speaking and hearing."
43. Beavis, Mark, 125.
44. Strauss, Mark, 322.
45. Earlier in this chapter we looked at Isa. 35:5, which talks about the ears of the deaf being unstopped. Isaiah 35:6 reads, "Then will the lame leap like a deer, and the mute tongue shout for joy."

won't be able to go to Pharaoh on Israel's behalf because he is "slow of speech and tongue" (Exod. 4:10). God reminds Moses that he is the one who oversees all sensory abilities. Jesus, in giving this man hearing and speech, embodies the authority of God.[46]

In response to this remarkable turn of events, everyone is amazed. Thematic to Mark's narrative, Jesus commands silence and secrecy: *Shhh! Don't tell anyone.* But the more he does this, the more everyone keeps talking about it (not in a negative, gossipy way but in the positive sense of proclamation).[47] Everyone who hears about it praises Jesus: "He has done everything well. He even makes the deaf hear and the mute speak" (Mark 7:37). I can't imagine how the man, especially, could stay quiet!

There seem to be fewer instances in the Gospels where Jesus heals those who lack hearing than those who lack sight. Robert Gundry suggests that restoring hearing was so "stupendous" that such occurrences were rather infrequent in the ancient world.[48] Like those without sight, those without hearing would have lived on the margins of society. Those without speech would have less opportunity to advocate for themselves and others. Certainly, for Jesus to restore any sensory ability would have furnished someone with expanded opportunity to participate in their respective communities. What a happy occasion! Now it's true, within the context, each healing was temporary; everyone who was healed by Jesus eventually died. But it's worth reflecting on how in these jubilant moments of restoration Jesus injects hope. Such healings, as Mark Strauss observes, provide "snapshots" of a future reality when the kingdom is realized and creation is restored.[49]

Hearing in the Fourth Gospel

As we "saw" in the previous chapter, the Fourth Gospel is rather sight-centric. John's prologue (John 1:1–18) kicks things off with the

---

46. Strauss, *Mark*, 323.
47. Strauss, *Mark*, 323.
48. Gundry, *Mark*, 384.
49. Strauss, *Mark*, 325.

Logos, "the Word," who was with God in the beginning. At first it might seem as if this is going to take us in a verbal direction: Don't we *hear* words spoken? But Jesus "the Word" is immediately described as "the light" that shines in the darkness (1:5). By the time we get to the Word becoming flesh (1:14), John is leaning on visual metaphors to convey this revelation.

But if you listen closely, there is a prominent theme of "testimony" woven throughout the Fourth Gospel from early on. While John says that no one has ever *seen* God (1:18), he also says that Jesus "makes him known," which carries verbal tones: Jesus explains and interprets God to the world. Jesus's words will testify throughout the Gospel to who he is, as Deborah Forger states: "Jesus's words concretize Israel's God."[50] John the Baptizer, for example, has listened for Jesus (3:29) and steps in as the Isaianic voice of one calling in the wilderness (1:23) to proclaim his arrival. John's voice joins others who together contribute a significant audible tone to this Gospel. Let's notice how hearing and speaking function as prominent metaphors for revealing God and inviting belief.

Hearing Jesus to Know God

John consistently postures Jesus, the Word made flesh, as the walking, talking, accessible embodiment of God. He alone can see and hear God (6:46; 12:28–29), which means that he's the only one who can reveal the Father (1:18): he speaks God's words (8:28; 12:49; 14:24) and walks in alignment with God's deeds (5:19). So, if we want to know God, we must listen to Jesus's voice.

But it's not enough just to hear it. Similar to the Synoptic Jesus's words—"Whoever has ears to hear, let them hear"—John's Jesus talks about what it means to *really* hear. In John's world, hearing rightly will result in following Jesus; these are believers set on the trajectory of eternal life (5:24). As Dorothy Lee puts it, "To hear means, for John, to recognize the Word (*logos*) in the words (*logoi*)."[51] Now, there are also some in John's Gospel who hear and do not believe

50. Forger, "Jesus as God's Word(s)," 276. She discusses how Jesus's words—his speech—serve to make God known in a tangible, embodied, accessible way.
51. Lee, "Gospel of John and the Five Senses," 121.

(12:47). For example, at the end of Jesus's "bread of life" teaching there are disciples who decide that his words are too hard to accept, and ultimately, they walk away (6:60, 66). One can hear Jesus, but John will continually invite people to respond in belief.

Hearing the Good Shepherd

John is famous for using vivid imagery. One of his most well-known illustrations is set immediately following a scene we have already encountered. Just after Jesus's tense interaction with the religious leaders and their consternation over his healing the man born blind (John 9), Jesus paints a portrait of the best kind of leader for God's people. He goes on to identify himself as that leader, saying, "I am the good shepherd" (10:11, 14). Notice how this is not a still-life portrait but one animated with lots of movement—including sound.

In the Scriptures familiar to the earliest Gospel communities, leaders of Israel are consistently compared to shepherds leading flocks of sheep (e.g., Num. 27:17). Such leaders include God and Messiah as shepherd (Ps. 95:7; Ezek. 34). These passages also address shepherds of Israel who do not care well for the sheep—there are strong warnings for those who are careless, neglectful, and downright abusive.

Jesus describes the ideal shepherd in an early morning village scene. As he arrives to lead the sheep out to pasture, the shepherd is welcomed through the gate by the gatekeeper (10:2–3a). The shepherd proceeds by calling his sheep by name, and the sheep follow the sound of his voice (10:3b–4). The shepherd's primary role in caring for the sheep is to find pasture for his flock. As the seasons grow warmer, this necessitates that they travel farther from home. At night, shepherds lead sheep into wilderness enclosures built from caves or created with stones. These structures typically had no roof or door, and the entrance was the most vulnerable opening for sheep. Often the shepherd laid across the entrance to protect the sheep by night (which helps us make sense of Jesus's adjacent claim, "I am the gate" [10:7]).

Sheep are quite vulnerable, often subject to illegitimate leaders. These leaders are compared to ill-intentioned thieves who steal, kill,

and destroy. Thieves usually try to sneak in by some illicit way—
like over the wall. But they will fail to get the sheep to follow them
simply because sheep won't recognize a stranger's voice (10:5). In
fact, sheep will run away from unfamiliar voices. The problem is
that even if sheep are not taken down by thieves, they are still sus-
ceptible to attack by predatory animals. This is particularly scary
when sheep are being cared for by a hired hand (10:12). The hired
hand is not nearly as invested as the shepherd and will flee at the
first sign of danger.

This is important: what binds the sheep to their shepherd is hearing the sound of his voice.[52] This embodied interaction is their pas-
sageway to safety and abundant life. The shepherd calls his sheep by
name, and as long as they respond by staying near to their leader's
voice, they can't go wrong. They will be led into "life to the full"
(10:10).

Jesus mentions that he wants to include sheep from other sheep-
folds. As he gathers them all together in one flock, Jesus compares
his knowledge of his sheep to his own connection to his Father, which
is a relationship marked by love (10:14–17).[53] This is a love modeled
after the love shared by Jesus and the Father.

Soon Jesus bends this illustration into a cruciform shape. The good
shepherd goes so far as to "lay down his life for the sheep" (10:11).
This stretches the metaphor quite a bit since if a shepherd dies, he
leaves sheep more exposed to danger.[54] Jesus here is pointing to his
coming death and resurrection, saying, "I lay [my life] down of my
own accord. I have authority to lay it down and authority to take it
up again" (10:18). This christological direction begins to take shape
in the wider Johannine narrative as very soon we encounter the events
leading up to the cross. Within the shepherding scene, John reminds
us that a shepherd leads a life of risk.[55] Remarkably, we are about
to see this very dynamic lived out in Jesus's own life. This is a risk
borne from love.

---

52. Kysar ("Johannine Metaphor," 90) notes that the sheep and the shepherd are
bound together by the theme of the shepherd's voice.

53. Bailey, Good Shepherd, 231.

54. Bultmann, John, 370–71n5.

55. Hylen, "Shepherd's Risk," 384; Bailey, Good Shepherd, 229.

Hearing the Sounds of Life

In the very next scene, Jesus is summoned by dear friends to go to Bethany, a town not very far from Jerusalem. Martha and Mary's brother, Lazarus, had become ill. They must have hoped that Jesus would come heal him. As this well-known story goes, Jesus arrives too late. Lazarus has been dead four days, and he has already been secured within the family tomb.

Notice how Martha and Mary each approach Jesus with identical opening words of regret: "If you had been here, my brother would not have died" (11:21, 32). They are devastated. They are close with Jesus, so they must have assumed that he would show up. Martha converses with Jesus about this, and he makes a bold claim: "I am the resurrection and the life" (11:25).[56] When Jesus asks if she believes these words, she says yes, but probably with a sense of internal resignation, assuming that Jesus is talking about the future resurrection.

When Mary encounters Jesus she crumples into a ball of tears. Her grief is deeply moving to Jesus. John uses an uncommon Greek word to describe Jesus's emotional state: it's a heartache that involves pain and grief but is also tinged with anger (11:33). As Jesus experiences the effects of the fallen world firsthand—a world subject to sickness, death, and sin—he is angry. Humanity is continually confronted with this kind of brokenness and loss, and here Jesus embraces our plight.[57] The mourners invite Jesus to "come and see" where Lazarus is entombed, and at this point Jesus also breaks down and weeps (11:35). Despite the fact that he knows he is about to raise Lazarus, Jesus carries such compassion for his friends that he has stepped inside the devastation wrought by the irreversible loss of death.

When they get to the tomb—I bet you know what's next—Jesus shocks everyone as he directs them to take the stone away from the entrance. In our next chapter we will return to this scene to inspect the smell that Martha is going to warn about. For now, let's imagine the audible quality of this scene. The dearly loved Lazarus has been

---

56. Note that this is the fifth of seven "I am" sayings that Jesus makes throughout John. We have already encountered the first four: "I am" the bread, the light, the gate, the good shepherd.

57. Klink (*John*, 508) calls this a "coparticipatory response."

laid to rest in the quietness of a dark, stone cave. The finality of death sounds like utter silence.

Jesus is about to interrupt this finality and its stillness. The by-standers take away the stone. That must have sounded eerily loud, and then silence settled in again. Any muffled weeping or murmuring about this turn of events is hushed by Jesus's prayer to the Father: "Father, I thank you that you have *heard* me. I know that you always *hear* me, but I said this for the benefit of those standing here, that they may *believe* that you sent me" (11:41–42). Notice the emphasis on hearing and belief.

Jesus's voice is about to bellow into the tomb and call Lazarus to come out. First, I want to draw your attention to an earlier passage in John's Gospel that mirrors this very scene; or perhaps it foreshadows it. It's pretty remarkable to see the parallels, as Jesus says this: "Very truly I tell you, a time is coming and has now come when the dead will *hear* the *voice* of the Son of God and those who *hear* will live. . . . Do not be amazed at this, for a time is coming when all who are in their graves will *hear* his *voice* and come out" (5:25, 28–29a). Have you ever thought about how Jesus is living out the shepherding illustration before our very eyes? He has claimed to be both the good shepherd and the resurrection and the life. In both "I am" metaphors the sheep are going to *hear* Jesus's *voice* calling them by name. Let's see how this plays out. In the following I am going to layer together all three passages—John 5, 10, and 11. Notice how hearing and speech figure in. Jesus, the Son of God and good shepherd (5:25; 10:11), *calls* his own sheep by name in a loud *voice* (10:3; 11:43), "Lazarus, come out!" The dead man (5:25; 11:44) in his grave (5:28) *hears* Jesus's *voice* (5:28), and lives (5:25; 10:10), and comes forth (5:29; 11:44).[58] In the complete stillness of the tomb, death is interrupted by the voice of the Son of God. I wonder how long it took before signs of life were seen and heard. Imagine the quiet at first. Then, Lazarus begins to emerge, slowly. Sounds of movement pierce the silence as he shuffles and struggles with his grave linens, across the threshold of the cave. Evidence of life is confounding in the place of death. Jesus has lived up to his claim; he is the resurrection and the life.

58. The layering of these passages is paired with a more detailed table that examines these passages side by side in Hanger, *Sensing Salvation*, 127, table 2.

The life of Lazarus puts the good shepherd's life at risk, as this event is the catalyst for Jesus's arrest and ultimate demise. Shortly after this scene we encounter Jesus's Farewell Discourse (John 13–17). This is a lengthy speech whereby Jesus reassures and instructs his disciples how they must go on once he is no longer bodily with them. These are words for disciples of all time—for you and me also. These are the words of the good shepherd, instructing his sheep on how to stay near and live the abundant life with him. All it takes on our part is attentive, responsive listening, the kind that *really* hears and follows.

Hearing for the Earliest Readers

As we consider the earliest ancient readers of these Gospel narratives, I want to take us back to the scenes where Jesus heals those who are deaf and mute. In his writing on the theology of disability, Amos Yong observes, "Because deafness was often understood by the ancients more in terms of intellectual rather than sensory impairment, deaf persons were assumed incapable of bearing legal responsibility and [therefore were] politically marginalized."[59] This resonates with our discussion in two ways. First, if this is true of the ancient world—that someone's lack of hearing subjected them to being misjudged as also lacking intellectual ability—then Jesus's restoration of their hearing would have affected more than their physical ability to hear. As with those to whom he gave sight, opening the ears of deaf persons would have created new opportunities for participation in their societal context and advocacy for themselves (and others) in ways that were not possible before. The multilayered effects of Jesus's healing gesture suggest the depth of his compassion to care for the whole person.

Second, if lack of hearing and speech had such a disabling effect in the ancient world, then this reminds us of the significance of this sensory ability in the ancient world. Hearing mattered. It was important. But if we take this into the register of "hearing Jesus," I want to suggest that hearing Jesus's voice—even if you don't have the physical capacity to hear—is possible. The following will explore how this plays out. As we've discussed, the high rank of hearing in

59. Yong, *Theology and Down Syndrome*, 28.

the ancient world is evidenced in how it was commonly linked with understanding, knowledge, and faith. As we consider Jesus's voice and the importance of hearing and heeding it, remember that to "really" hear Jesus's words indicates a quality of faith that characterizes a disciple of Jesus. If ancient readers can understand the sense of hearing in this symbolic register, then the ability to become someone who "really" hears Jesus's words is available to all, even to those who cannot physically hear very well.

Now, it's true that those with the ability to hear physically would have the benefit of a kind of embodied understanding of how "hearing the voice" of Jesus resembles a particular sound. And yet, as with sight, postresurrection ancient readers with their hearing intact probably would admit that they had never heard the audible voice of Jesus. So, as all of us are invited to consider the words of Jesus, note that to really "hear" them doesn't require actual physical hearing. This means that ancient readers were not much different from modern readers interacting with Jesus's voice. We all, like sheep, are privy to the words of the good shepherd, and we are all invited to decide: Will we follow his voice? Will we really hear it?

Reflections on Hearing for Modern Readers

Here we pick up on the thread of the previous section. To truly "hear" Jesus's voice doesn't necessitate physical hearing. We can engage with Jesus's words using multiple senses. We can hear the words of Jesus with our ears as they are spoken aloud, but we can also "hear" them as we read them on a page, with our eyes. Moreover, we can "hear" them within our minds and hearts as we mull them over. And let me give you a little *taste* of what's to come: What if Jesus's words are something we can touch? What if we can "hear" his words through smell? Obviously, I am talking about a proverbial sense of hearing, the kind of hearing that symbolizes receptivity. Do we have ears to hear the words of the Word? How will we respond?

Let's return to John's Gospel as we close out this chapter. John provides such a vivid picture—or maybe you can imagine a surround-sound feature film—demonstrating a tangible quality of life that believers-as-sheep can have with Jesus-as-shepherd. He is the *good* shepherd, who knows his sheep so well that he calls them by name. In fact, it's likely that he has named them himself, with fondness for each one. I wonder if sheep also resonate with affection at the sound of the shepherd's voice. Much like Frederick Douglass's embodied response to memories of melancholy songs, do we carry embodied responses to sounds, such as the familiar call of a beloved shepherd?

When Jesus calls his sheep, they are invited to follow. He will not lead them astray; he will find them food and water and a place to lie down at night. He will protect them from the elements, from predators, and from the threat of those who don't have the sheep's best interests at heart. In order for this sheep-shepherd relationship to sing, there is a unique blend of dependence and freedom that characterizes the salvific, abundant life. In other words, it is through the flock's persistent dependence on the shepherd—which looks like hearing his voice and staying near—that sheep experience the most liberty. Their freedom is born from their dependence, which, if you think about it in modern terms, sounds like a paradox.

In today's modern context, the concept of *in*dependence signals a kind of freedom. Our world of radical individualism trains us to live rather differently than sheep. Today it sounds completely backward to us to consider dependence to be an ideal state, much less a goal. But think about sheep. Their big goal in life is not to develop into independent, autonomous beings that graduate and venture out from the flock to make their mark on the world. Sheep never outgrow their dependence on the shepherd. I suspect that dependence is a key ingredient to our flourishing in God's economy, but this is quite different from what modern society promotes. I often wonder if championing independence and autonomy works against us as followers of Jesus. Does it shape and disciple our hearts away from a life of *really* hearing from God? Thriving sheep are those who depend on their shepherd, and it is this dependence that creates the most freedom and flourishing. But in addition to—even better than?—seeking flourishing for the sheep is the sweet goal of maintaining presence with the shepherd. Remember: this is the *good* shepherd, one who knows our names, whose every move has been fueled by his love. Why wouldn't we want to listen, depend, and stay close?

SNIPPETS OF SOUND
TO LEAD THE WAY

1. Sometimes we have to quiet the noise around us to really hear the voice of the Good Shepherd. Consider engaging in a short fast from the noise of your day-to-day life. Find a one-hour time *and* space where you can reside in silence. This can be accomplished in several ways: sitting in a quiet room, taking a walk outside, or going to an open space in nature. Silence (turn off and hide) your mobile devices. You may preface your time by briefly "listening to" (reading) the words of Scripture, but do not fill this space with reading. Take the following questions into this one-hour time of silence:

    a. How do you feel about the idea that the Good Shepherd knows your name?

    b. Do you believe that he wants to talk to you? If not, why not? If so, what is he saying to you in this season of your life?

    c. If you struggle to discern whether it is his voice or yours that you are listening to, consider this: his voice is often kinder than yours.

2. One of the ways we can hear God is to listen to his words to us in Scripture. For this exercise, choose a phrase that comes from God's heart and is confirmed by his Word, and commit to meditating on it purposefully over a length of time.

    a. What to meditate on: It can be a simple phrase, such as "I am God's beloved," or "Consider others first," or "His name is above every name," or "Perfect love drives out fear."

    b. How to do it: Commit to this exercise for one day, or for three days, or maybe even for a whole week. Write this phrase in several prominent places, such as in a journal or on your bathroom mirror. Set the phrase as an alarm on your phone that goes off every day at the same time. Let these reminders prompt you to repeat this phrase to yourself, whether quietly or out loud. Experiment with whatever helps you to keep this phrase top of mind.

3. The right kind of music can have a settling effect. Instead of fasting from noise, create a peaceful backdrop to spend an hour in the presence of the Lord. Create a playlist that can set the stage. Perhaps, for you, it needs to include meaningful lyrics. Or if lyrics are distracting, find some instrumental music. Does the music need to be calm and quiet, or will it encourage you if it's more upbeat? Decide how you want to spend this hour. Will you take a walk or find a comfy spot to sit? Construct an ideal setting for listening to the voice of God.

6

Smelling Death and Life

Jesus Makes Scents of Memorable Fragrance

In 2011 we moved our family across town into a new neighborhood, and one of the first things I did was establish a new running route. My running route is my lifeline: it's the ordinary, stable, fixed path that I can roll out of bed and settle into as a way of kick-starting my body for the day. It helps me maintain a level of psychological, emotional, and spiritual equilibrium in the midst of the stressors of life.

A couple years into logging miles on this route, I missed an early morning run and decided to run the course in the evening. You'd think it would be an identical experience—it was the same, boring, rectangular loop of suburbia. However, that evening I encountered something new. It was a new scent. Actually, what stopped me in my tracks wasn't that it was a new scent but that it was an *old* one. It was a *familiar* scent. When I first noticed it, I knew that I had smelled this scent before, because immediately I thought of Grandma Pera.

Maybe you have a "Grandma Pera" in your family. Grandma Pera was my dad's mother, who passed away when I was sixteen years old. Her given name was Victoria, but people called her Elsie (as one does, go figure). Growing up, Elsie was an important fixture in our loud, boisterous, loving, Italian extended family. Of course, Elsie was not the boisterous one; she was the warm, welcoming presence at our frequent gatherings on Sweetbriar Drive. She could always be found sitting at the head of the long dinner table opposite Grandpa Pera (Mario—definitely one of the loud ones). I will forever remember Elsie in her matriarchal perch, always with one elbow on the table, propping up her elegantly balanced cigarette. Of course, this was back in the day when we were learning how harmful smoking was for one's health, when setting out ashtrays for family gatherings was as common as offering ice buckets and bowls of peanuts. Stray grandkids always seemed drawn to Elsie's end of the table, where they milled around her orbit, angling for permission to open the cookie drawer.[1] Elsie always said yes to cookies. She always had a smile; she always laughed at the family's antics. Even though I was one of eleven grandchildren, I always felt special in her presence. If you asked each of her grandkids, they might say the same: *She made me feel special too*. We were all devastated when she passed away. It felt far too soon.

One time—I must have been about fifteen, because I was not quite old enough to drive and be in charge of my three younger siblings—we stayed at Elsie's house while our parents were away overnight. I'll never forget riding in her big, cream-colored boat of a car, a Ford Granada. The license plate read "ThaBigE" (for "Elsie," of course). Elsie took us to Round Table Pizza for dinner that night. There we encountered a cute boy eating pizza who was perhaps a bit too old to be giving attention to a young teenage girl. I didn't see the problem, but Elsie was not having it. We giggled as she peeled out of that Round Table parking lot in ThaBigE to get us away from this dangerous young man as fast as possible.

So, back to my evening run. It was there, on my same-old, same-old route that I could swear I scented Elsie herself. The moment literally

---

1. Yes, there was an *entire* kitchen drawer dedicated to cookies. Someday I am going to have one of these in my house!

took my breath away. But where was it coming from? I looked around at what was different. And then I saw it: the local alehouse. Typically shuttered in the morning, by night the doors were flung open, with patrons spilling out onto the sidewalk. There is something in the depths of that historic establishment—I suspect it's the stale cigarette smoke embedded into an old carpet—that gives off serious Elsie vibes. Taking in that stale but precious scent, I felt like I was fifteen again, riding in ThaBigE with sweet Elsie Pera, speeding away from Round Table.

By now you must think me a bit quirky. Who cherishes inhaling big gulps of dusty cigarette air? *Me. I do.* I'm not embarrassed to admit that the highlight of any evening run is passing by that alehouse. I actually slow down and angle my gait as close to the entrance as I can, just so I can take a long, nostalgic pull on that smoky aroma. In one breath, in a singular, momentary smell, I am a child again at the Sweetbriar house, when Elsie was alive and welcoming me into her embrace, protecting me from dangerous cute boys.

Throughout this chapter we will consider the significance of the olfactory sense. Smells are potent, in part because they carry connections in our brains to memory and emotion. This is why a scent can immediately transport us to the past. Smell is quite useful. It serves as a warning, such as when you catch a whiff of burnt rubber while driving on the freeway. *Is something wrong with my car?* Or when you smell something sour in the kitchen. *Has the milk gone bad?*

But despite its potency and usefulness, smell is often neglected. Perhaps it has something to do with its invisibility, its soundlessness. Smells often waft through the air, covertly sneaking into our awareness. Suddenly you are tilting your head and thinking to yourself, *What is that smell?* Some scents we all know—like the aroma of coffee brewing or the distinct odor of a skunk—while other smells take us a minute to recognize.

Hence, "waft-y" smells are easy to overlook, and they are especially absent from written texts, which you are about to see evidence of as we survey the Gospels. Smell is the physical sense mentioned the *least*. But it doesn't mean it's missing from the setting. And it certainly doesn't mean that it's unimportant. Before we venture into a conversation about the scents of the Gospels, let's explore the anatomy and history of smell.

Insights on Smell

Back in the 1990s, sociology professor and sensory researcher Anthony Synnott conducted an informal survey of 183 students about how they would rank their sense perceptions. He asked them, if forced to choose, which sense they would sacrifice first. About 57 percent of students reported they would say goodbye to smell first, followed by taste.[2] Many suggested that smell was useful only for protecting oneself against burning toast.[3] Perhaps the loss of smell is little more than an inconvenience? But what if there's more to it than that?

The Complex Presence of Smell

Synnott discusses several factors involving how we underestimate smell. First, smell is often overlooked because of the supremacy of sight.[4] Second, the low status of smell correlates with how little it's been studied. Think about the lack of vocabulary we have for smell.[5] We often describe scents according to words we use for taste: this smells *sweet* or *sour*; or according to words for touch: this coffee is *strong* or *weak*. Third, smell is undervalued simply because it can be associated with bad odors. Humans are constantly trying to get rid of (or mask) our natural human odors.[6] Smell is frequently associated with animalistic behavior because animals depend on smell more than we do.

---

2. Synnott, *The Body Social*, 183.

3. Synnott, *The Body Social*, 183. Of course, in 2020 we lived out a version of Synnott's experiment when the global pandemic witnessed multitudes of people lose the sense of smell (*and* taste) while infected with the COVID-19 virus. Anecdotally, it seems that grappling with the (mostly) temporary loss of smell was less dire than the loss of touch (social distance and isolation). For more, see Duke Health News Office, "Why Loss of Smell Can Persist after COVID-19," News & Research, Harvard Medical School, December 21, 2022, https://hms.harvard.edu/news/why-loss-smell -can-persist-after-covid-19.

4. Synnott, *The Body Social*, 183.

5. Synnott, *The Body Social*, 184.

6. Synnott, *The Body Social*, 185.

In recent years smell is perhaps gaining more attention. The fragrance industry is big business, after all.[7] Consider that "fragrance" goes beyond monies spent on perfumes: there are innumerable scents curated in and emitted by deodorants, detergents, air fresheners, candles, oil diffusers, and foods. These cultural trends suggest that to a certain extent fragrance is important to daily life, even if we don't tend to reflect on it.

The Anatomy of Smell

In Aristotle's sense hierarchy, smell falls exactly in the middle.[8] It's a close neighbor to the higher-classed sight and hearing and to the lower-classed taste and touch, with similarities and differences with both groups. For example, smell functions like sight and hearing as a distanced sense, since aroma travels with color and sound through the air to our perceptive faculties. However, unlike sight and hearing, smell is not typically linked with philosophy and understanding. Instead, it tends to resemble taste and touch as being more rudimentary and "animalistic."[9]

Neuroscientists like Venki Murthy talk about how the anatomy of smell influences taste. When you chew food, the molecules travel "retro-nasally" to the nasal epithelium such that "all of what you consider flavor is smell."[10] This is why pinching the nose can cut out much of the taste of a given food while eating.

7. In 1993 Synnott (*The Body Social*, 182) reported fragrance sales in the United States alone to be valued at around $3.5 billion, while today market research companies value the fragrance and perfume industry at around $61 billion globally, with the US representing less than 20 percent of that number ("Fragrance & Perfume Industry Size & Share Analysis—Growth Trends & Forecasts (2023–2028)," Mordor Intelligence, accessed December 19, 2023, https://www.mordorintelligence.com/industry-reports/fragrance-and-perfume-market).

8. Aristotle, *On the Soul* 5.445a7–10.

9. Philo, *On Abraham* 29.149.

10. The following information on smell is based on a lecture given by Venkatesh (Venki) Murthy, professor of molecular and cellular biology, Harvard University, in "Olfaction in Science and Society," sponsored by the Harvard Museum of Natural History in collaboration with the Harvard Science Initiative. The full discussion is available at https://www.youtube.com/watch?v=J-LQoqBQ8T4. It was reported and summarized by Walsh, "What the Nose Knows."

How does smell operate? Murthy explains that fragrant objects release chemicals whose molecules travel through the air into our breath-space.[11] We inhale these molecules through the nose into the nasal epithelium, where they are processed by neurons, which send electrical signals into the olfactory bulb of the brain. It is through these electrical signals that we perceive smell. But even more complex, as these electrical signals enter the brain, they go immediately into the limbic system, the center for emotion and memory. Scientists are still trying to trace and decipher the various feedback loops that these signals travel in order to understand the connections between smell, memory, and emotion.

The plot thickens even more. Scientists have discovered how a person's sense of smell is fully developed as early as thirteen weeks in utero, and it serves as the "dominant and primary" sense until someone is about ten years old (when sight takes over). With this finding, olfactive branding expert Dawn Goldworm discusses the collaborative relationship between smell and emotion in these early years.[12] They are so tightly connected that whenever we have an emotional experience, the smell that is present at the time becomes associated with that event. Once this link is established in the brain, it creates an olfactive memory. Each of us grows up with our own collection of olfactive experiences that determine the smells we like and the smells we dislike for the rest of our lives. This is how, in my case, stale cigarette smoke is a pleasant, nostalgic smell, associated with core memories tied to positive emotions.[13]

All of this suggests that smell is more significant than we give it credit for. Smell is silent and invisible but is not to be discounted, as it can exert considerable influence on us personally. From here let's consider how it plays into the social, cultural, and spiritual dynamics of daily life, in both the modern and ancient worlds.

11. Murthy, in Walsh, "What the Nose Knows."

12. Goldworm curates signature fragrances for celebrity personalities and for companies like Nike, joining Murthy as a panel contributor to share the fruits of her research in the discussion. Goldworm and Murthy, "Olfaction in Science and Society."

13. Goldworm shares about a lecture during which she gave a sample of the smell of gasoline to a young woman in the audience, which triggered surprisingly good feelings for her because it reminded her of pleasant childhood memories growing up in New York City.

Smell in Modern and Ancient Contexts

Much of the territory covered so far has been focused on brain science and how smell operates in the register of the individual, embodied person. Now, let's reintroduce the cultural dynamics of smell, especially since we know that science is also culturally mediated.[14] While it is safe to say that smells can be universally experienced, remember that how we value smell varies across individuals *and* cultures. The following will consider some general cultural differences between the value of smell in modern versus ancient contexts.

To a large extent, modern Western society tends to overlook smell. That's how we opened our discussion: we have highlighted smell's potency, and yet we tend to neglect it. Part of this disregard can be traced to distinct shifts occurring in the wake of the "olfactive revolution" originating in European society in the eighteenth and nineteenth centuries. One of these shifts was the development of the autonomous self. Birthed in part from the Kantian concept of "moral autonomy," this more-modern iteration of individualism prized self-determination over submitting oneself to the injunctions of others. With this emerging sense of "self"-consciousness came heightened awareness of individual body odors.[15] This in turn led people in the West to be less tolerant of others' bodily smells, culminating in a society seeking to eradicate smell altogether. As E. T. Hall observes, "The extensive use of deodorants and the suppression of odours in public places results in a land of olfactory blandness and sameness that would be difficult to duplicate anywhere else in the world."[16] With this trend of olfactory "silence," we have reached a point where, as William Ian Miller states, "the best smell is not a good smell but no smell at all."[17]

14. We do share some universal realities about smell. However, a culture's valuation of the senses influences how smell is studied scientifically. Recall chapter 1, where we discussed the Andaman Islanders, who prioritize smell over other senses. Within their context it seems possible that they would socialize their children to interact with smell differently than other cultures do. How might this influence brain development in their community?

15. Howes, "Olfaction and Transition," 412.

16. Hall, *Hidden Dimension*, 45.

17. Miller, "Darwin's Disgust," 349. Of course, we don't live in completely odor-free spaces. Part of how we eliminate culturally "unacceptable" smells is by masking

To contrast this, the ancient world was likely a more fragrant environment. Recalling chapter 1, let's address two things. First, dominant social groups were linked to the highly ranked senses, while more inferior groups were linked to the "lower" senses, including smell. So, men were associated with sight and hearing, since their activities revolved around being out in a sight- and audio-centric world, while women were linked to the homebound senses of smell, taste, and touch.[18]

Second—and this is framed in terms of smell, even though other senses display this dynamic—social rank was linked to certain valuations of smells. The higher the social rank, the more pleasant the smell. "Good" smells were associated with wealthier economic classes, while "negative" smells were associated with those of lesser economic means. Smells were directly related to certain trades; people literally smelled like their occupations. Manual laborers, such as tanners and fullers, carried the stench of their day of work.[19] Not only that but the wealthy could afford to mask negative smells in their world using oils, perfumes, and so forth.[20]

Smell was linked to gender in complex ways. First, women were more often associated with negative smells than men were.[21] But also, certain *types* of women—those considered more desirable—were regarded as more pleasantly fragrant. Young women smelled better than old women, attractive and well-born women smelled better than less attractive or poor women, and moral women smelled better than "immoral" women—such as those employed in brothels.[22]

---

over them with other, more culturally "pleasant," manufactured smells. Yet this in itself is a fairly subjective endeavor. As Macaskill (*Autism and the Church*, 22, 28) points out, some manufactured odors designed to mask natural smells can be quite unpleasant for some, such as those with autism. For many, these engineered scents "smell *painfully*."

18. Howes, introduction to *Empire of the Senses*, 10.

19. Aldrete ("Urban Sensations," 53) talks about how tanneries were located in marginalized parts of town due to the odorous fumes they emitted. Fullers conducted their work of laundering clothing by collecting jars of urine throughout the city and by employing people (often slaves) to tread on the clothing in large vats of it.

20. Aldrete, "Urban Sensations," 52, citing examples from Pliny, *Natural History* 13.2.4–13.5.25.

21. Classen, Howes, and Synnott, *Aroma*, 36, 38.

22. Toner, "Sensing the Ancient Past," 7.

Today we formulate similar kinds of value judgments, although they play out differently. Going forward, I invite you to consider how we link smells to gender, or economics, or morality, in our own contexts.

Sacred Scents

One of the aspects of scent we have yet to address is how it wafts into conversations about spirituality. In the earliest centuries of the Christian church, aroma was believed to carry a sacred quality.[23] For example, it was believed that fragrant smells were emitted by revered saints and holy leaders, particularly at death. Susan Ashbrook Harvey highlights how, in the martyrdom of Polycarp (AD 155), smell helped to describe and recast his death as noble.[24] According to Christian witnesses, Polycarp's burning flesh smelled like baking bread, and the air had the quality of fragrant incense, the aroma of a pleasing sacrifice before God.[25] As Harvey suggests, fragrance has played a role in the construction of early Christian identity.

Scents in Scripture

As I've been hinting at, the mention of smell is not prevalent in the Gospels or in other parts of Scripture. Where it does appear, it is significant. In 2 Corinthians 2:14–16, Paul uses smell as a metaphor to describe how God uses us to spread the *aroma* of the knowledge of him everywhere: "For we are to God the pleasing *aroma* of Christ among those who are being saved and those who are perishing. To the one we are an *aroma* that brings death; to the other, an *aroma*

23. Classen, "Breath of God," 375. She writes, "The Christian concept of the odor of sanctity had its roots in the aromatic myths and rituals of the ancient world" (379).

24. Harvey, *Scenting Salvation*, 11. Polycarp was burned at the stake in Smyrna for refusing to sacrifice to Roman gods, and, as the story goes, when his body was not consumed, his executioners stabbed him. This event is described in the Martyr-dom of Polycarp, which is believed to have been written in Smyrna and circulated to other churches.

25. Harvey, *Scenting Salvation*, 12. Classen ("Breath of God," 376–77) highlights similar "sanctified" odors of other saints, such as, in the sixteenth century, the sweet-smelling postmortem coffin of St. Francis Xavier, and St. Teresa of Avila, fragrant in her sicknesses, death, and postburial.

that brings life." Here smell is linked to the knowledge of Christ in a way that elevates it to the realm of spiritual reflection.[26]

Yael Avrahami points out the dearth of references to smell in the Hebrew Bible but does highlight several. For example, scent is narrated into the events surrounding Jacob stealing Esau's blessing (Gen. 27:27). It was the smell of Jacob's garments that deceived Isaac, with the potency of scent magnified in the absence of Isaac's sight. His words even combine the two senses: "*See*, the *smell* of my son is as the *smell* of a field which the LORD has blessed!" (RSV).[27] Despite the rare linguistic appearance of smell in the Hebrew Bible, Avrahami notices such synaesthetic combinations between both smell and sight, and smell and taste.

Smell in the Synoptics

New Testament scholar Brittany Wilson explores the connection between smell and sacrifice in Luke-Acts.[28] She illustrates how Luke 1 evokes the sense of smell within the context of the Jewish sacrificial cult, and yet—important for our purposes—it does so implicitly. Smell is present but, true to form, invisible and silent, both in the narrative scene and in the text itself. Anything evoking a smell must be imagined as we step inside the scene.

This Synoptics section will consist of an aromatic "flyover" tour. This in part reflects how seldom smell and fragrance are featured—which is to say that smell is basically not mentioned at all. However, as Wilson demonstrates in her study, smell is implicit. And, I would add, this presence is rather pervasive throughout the contexts of these stories. In other words, smell is the silent and invisible character present in many scenes. During this flyover, I invite you to imagine the most potentially fragrant parts of the story, considering how smell operates in each scene.

26. Attridge ("Making Scents of Paul," 88) provides a stimulating discussion of the various dynamics wrapped into Paul's use of scent.

27. Avrahami, *Senses of Scripture*, 103. Additional examples include the exodus narrative (Exod. 5:21 NRSVue) and Absalom's rebellion against his father, David (2 Sam. 16:21 RSV).

28. Wilson, "Smell of Sacrifice."

The following will be structured according to four theoretically fragrant settings.[29] These are the temple, households, banquets, and burials. Our first example further examines Wilson's study in Luke 1, which takes place in the temple setting.

The Temple and Zechariah's Fragrant Offering

Wilson explores the very first scene in Luke's Gospel, when Zechariah is chosen by lot to go to the Jerusalem temple to burn incense (Luke 1:5–20). This is a rare opportunity for Zechariah to step into an established, long-standing, twice-daily worship ritual located at the center of Jewish cultic practice. Every day, morning and afternoon, the Jews observed this liturgy involving a lamb, oil, flour, and trumpets.[30] Luke draws attention to another element of this service, the offering of "incense." Luke conspicuously mentions this fragrant term three times (1:9, 10, 11).

Notably, this implied fragrance is emitted in the context of worship. Wilson observes that Zechariah is standing in a sacred location, almost as close as anyone can get to the very presence of God.[31] Imagine how the smell of incense might have filled this sanctuary and drifted through its crevices to reach other worshipers on the outside. This is the fragrance of divine connection.

Wilson observes two interruptions that indicate that God is doing something new.[32] Gabriel's announcement interrupts Zechariah's fragrant incense offering,[33] and the silencing of Zechariah halts the remainder of the liturgy. By drawing attention to the fragrant quality

29. Wilson ("Smell of Sacrifice," 259n5) mentions the work of Anne Elvey (*Matter of the Text*, 110–15), who pinpoints these four settings throughout Luke where fragrance-rich elements are mentioned, implying scented environments.

30. This is known as the Tamid service, detailed in Mishnah tractate Tamid. Hamm ("Tamid Service," 216) notes that within the postexilic Jewish imagination, the Tamid service would have formed the "primary liturgy of the temple."

31. Wilson, "Smell of Sacrifice," 262. Zechariah is in the sanctuary of the temple, just outside the holy of holies, which was open only to the high priest on the yearly Day of Atonement.

32. Wilson, "Smell of Sacrifice," 274.

33. Wilson notices how the other sensory elements eclipse the aroma: Gabriel *appears*, and Zechariah is afraid when he *sees* him. Gabriel *speaks*; Zechariah's prayer had been *heard*. After Zechariah expresses doubt, he is unable to *speak*.

of this practice—and its interruptions—Wilson observes how Luke turns our attention "away from the smells of the Jewish sacrificial system" to announce new life, to introduce Jesus.[34]

At the center of Jewish sacred life was the temple, where people came near to God, and it also was the location of customary, calendrical pilgrimage. Here sacrifices were offered, festivals celebrated, and incense burned. Worshipers visiting the temple would have encountered fragrance, creating olfactive memories connected to their embodied devotion to God.

Households

All three Gospels talk about the time when Jesus and his disciples come to the home of Simon and Andrew. Here they encounter Simon's mother-in-law, feverish and bedridden. Jesus takes her hand and helps her up, and the fever leaves her. Then she begins to wait on them (Mark 1:31).[35] Presuming a household in which *waiting on them* involves extending hospitality to her guests, it wouldn't be a stretch to suggest that preparation of food is involved. Mark reports that after sunset, people bring to Jesus all the sick and demon-possessed (1:32), as "the whole town gathered at the door" (1:33). Jesus conducts his healing ministry right out of Simon and Andrew's home.

I love imagining this household setting. At some point after Simon's mother-in-law is healed, she must have rejoined others to cook dinner for this small band of disciples. This means that the backdrop for Jesus's evening healing session not only involves fellowship amid friends but also includes the smells of home: the remnants of food roasted on a fire, fresh-baked bread, and sweet wine. What a fitting atmosphere for what comes next, as Jesus welcomes the town to their doorstep and works miracles before everyone's eyes. Notice how Jesus ministers not in formal, "sacred" locations but rather in the comforts of someone's safe, personal space, shared with others.

Let's remember the time when Martha opened her home to Jesus (Luke 10:38–42). We don't have much to go on, and smell is not

---

34. Wilson, "Smell of Sacrifice," 264.
35. See also Matt. 8:14–17; Luke 4:38–41.

mentioned. But if Martha is frustrated that Mary is not helping with *all the preparations*, my guess is that there are aromas from a meal in the works. As we know, Jesus affirms Mary for sitting at his feet. I've always wondered what happened next: Did Martha have to cook the whole meal by herself? More likely, Jesus is simply unconcerned with its timing; perhaps they ate later than Martha planned. It would fit Jesus's character to invite Martha to take a seat next to her sister to learn from him too. Afterward, what if everyone—women *and* men—pitched in to put dinner on the table that night? Of course, Luke doesn't record any of this, and I'm not trying to add to Scripture; it's just imaginative wondering. But do you notice—as in the story of Simon's mother-in-law—how women are associated with activities of the home (and, by implication, its scents)? It seems significant that Jesus teaches disciples out on the road and surrounded by the aromas of homes.

Banquets

Jesus is narrated as attending many banquets, and since we've discussed these in chapter 3, the treatment here will be brief. Think of the aromas involved when the newly minted disciple Levi hosts a dinner and Jesus eats with his notorious friends, the tax collectors and "sinners" (Mark 2:15; Luke 5:29). Another time, on the Sabbath Jesus is invited to eat dinner at the house of a prominent Pharisee (Luke 14:1–14). Here he heals a man suffering from abnormal swelling on his body, and he then shares a parable about the kingdom as a wedding feast. Where there's food, there's aroma, which means that these banquets would have been deliciously fragrant events.

All four Gospels narrate how Jesus is anointed with fragrant perfume by a woman during a meal (Matt. 26:6–13; Mark 14:3–9; Luke 7:36–50; John 12:1–8).[36] John's is the only telling where fragrance is literally mentioned, and we will address his narration below. In the

---

36. Matthew and Mark seem to describe the same anointing as John, while Luke may be talking about a different woman altogether since she is described as a sinner who comes crying at Jesus's feet. Luke's anointing is at a Pharisee's house earlier in Jesus's ministry, interpreted not as a burial anointing but as an opportunity to talk about love for Jesus and the forgiveness he extends.

Synoptics, a woman pours perfume on Jesus from an alabaster jar.[37] As with Zechariah's incense offering, smell is only implied, but the mere mention of this perfume suggests a strong fragrance. Mark says that she "broke" the jar. Think of the fragrance, radiating out among the dinner guests, with no way to put the strong smell back into the bottle.

The clue that fragrance plays a significant role in this story is the protest that her gesture sparks: *What a waste!* the disciples complain. Jesus predicts that her gesture will be told in her memory (Matt. 26:13; Mark 14:9). Think about the *olfactive* memory that this surprising anointing creates for those witnessing the fragrant scene. Future encounters with this fragrance will bring this event to mind, fulfilling Jesus's prediction as the story is retold.

Perhaps the aromas of these banquets seem decorative, especially where smell is not mentioned. But if smell is as memorable as we've said, it's worth considering its role in carrying memories of these traditions along: from eyewitness, to oral tradition, to written words. Let's move to our final odiferous setting.

Burials and Near-Burials

Anthropologist David Howes presents a fascinating study exploring how smells hover around transitions. Smell, he says, can be instrumental in signaling a shift that is underway. This is because smell occupies a unique liminal space; it has a way of "escaping" from its object and can be in more than one place at a time. As such, smell ushers along a process of transition.[38]

Think, for example, about how the aroma of food can mark the beginning of the dinner hour as it escapes from the kitchen and floats into the living room. It lets you know that food is cooking and dinnertime is approaching.[39] At the sociological, communal level, scents like incense can hover in the transition of preparing congregations for engaging in worship and heightening spiritual fervor.[40] Olfaction is

---

37. Matthew and Mark report her anointing his head, Luke and John his feet.
38. Howes, "Olfaction and Transition," 404.
39. Howes, "Olfaction and Transition," 401–2.
40. Howes, "Olfaction and Transition," 403.

also involved in various rites of passage, such as when boys transition into manhood or girls into womanhood. Relevant to this conversation, smells exist among a culture's funerary traditions, helping to usher someone to their final resting place.

Going from life to death occurs in a moment and can be perceived as final and abrupt. But consider the process that we walk through and how long it takes to acclimate to the fact that a loved one is no longer with us. Over time we change our thinking as this beloved person transitions from being alive among us to cherished ancestor. Howes describes this intermediary period and how odor helps usher a body to its final rest. For some societies, "death is a process which is not complete until the corpse has reached a skeletal condition."[41]

In the Synoptics, there are several places where Jesus encounters those who have died. In these occurrences, smell is never mentioned. But again, as we know, smells are everywhere. They hover as we sit vigil by someone's deathbed. When this person passes away, we have spent time watching, listening, speaking, holding hands, and smelling as we share presence, wait, and say our goodbyes. Before long, the smell of death sets in as the body begins the phases of decomposition.

One time, a synagogue leader named Jairus comes to Jesus in dire need (Matt. 9:18–26; Mark 5:21–43; Luke 8:40–56). His twelve-year-old daughter lies dying. Would Jesus come, he asks, and put his hand on her so that she might live? But by the time Jesus arrives it is too late, and she has passed away. When Jesus enters the house, the sounds of mourning have commenced, with weeping and wailing (Mark 5:38; Luke 8:52) and pipes playing (Matt. 9:23). Before too long Jesus takes her hand and restores her to life and to her parents. I'd guess that the smell of death has not set in just yet.

In the previous chapter we explored the voice of Jesus raising the widow's son just outside the city gate of Nain (Luke 7:11–17). Notice how the setting for this event is the man's funerary procession. When Jesus stops the crowd, the son is being carried on a bier, presumably to his final resting place. His body probably has been prepared for burial with spices. If the odor of decomposition is beginning to set

---

41. Howes, "Olfaction and Transition," 405.

in, it would be paired with these fragrant burial aromatics. If this bier is in the middle of two converging crowds, perhaps this smell of death emanates among the people while they witness Jesus's voice call life out of death. What an interesting clash of sights, sounds, and smells! Jesus interrupts the transition of the body from corpse to skeletal ancestor, and I'm guessing that instead of proceeding to the cemetery, everyone returns to town to celebrate new life.

Our fragrant tour of the Synoptics has drawn to a close. While these four settings—temple, household, banquet, and burial—can only offer implicit scents, I hope that this discussion has sparked your imagination. The more we can "get inside" a narrative, the more we realize that (even implicit) smells contribute value as we consider the fully embodied qualities of each scene. As we turn to the Fourth Gospel, I am excited to explore with you some of the more explicit appearances of smell.

Smell in the Fourth Gospel

I could take us on a fantastic fragrant flyover tour of the implicit smells in John, but this is the only Gospel that explicitly mentions smell. So, we will focus on these occurrences, with some implied aromas figured into the discussion where relevant. There are two scenes in which smell appears, and what makes these stand out even more is how they correlate with each other. Both smells hover specifically around themes of life and death.

In today's world, most of us don't really know what death smells like.[42] We largely rely on "professionals"—coroners, embalmers, funeral directors—to come in and prepare a body for its final resting place. Simple technology like refrigeration mitigates the stench of death for even these professionals. In the ancient world, there was much more exposure to death, its decomposition, and its stench. Families were more often involved in preparing bodies for burial.[43]

---

42. For those who grew up in rural settings, that might provide more context for the smell of death due to more frequent encounters with the deaths of animals.

43. Josephus (*Against Apion* 2.205) mentions that family and friends conducted funerary rites.

They would know—at least more than we do today—what death smells like.

According to Jewish custom, when someone died, his or her body was prepared for burial by bathing and anointing it with aromatic ointments. Often this was conducted in the family home.[44] After this, the body was wrapped in strips of linen and carried on a bier to be buried, much like the widow's son in Luke 7:11–17. If a family could afford it, the body would be set into a rock-cut tomb with a stone laid across the entrance. The tomb would be located at a distance from the space of the living. Three days later, relatives would return and treat the body with more spices and perfumes.[45] Imagine the smells that a tomb would collect as this planned distance helps usher the body through its transition into the ancestral memory that Howes talks about.

Life from the Stench of Death

Now, think back to the previous chapter when we explored the raising of Lazarus (John 11:1–44). There we focused on the utter silence of the death tomb and how Jesus's booming voice startles Lazarus to life. When he hears the shepherd's voice calling his name, Lazarus emerges across the threshold of the tomb, piercing the silence of death with sounds of life. He is the sheep following the voice of the good shepherd, through the gate into abundant life.

Let's return to this scene, focusing on the role of smell. As Jesus asks to see the tomb, notice how Lazarus's burial arrangements follow the custom of separation between home and tomb, helping the family to proceed through a grieving farewell to their beloved brother.[46] Jesus interrupts this trajectory when he directs the mourners to take away the stone. Martha protests: "Lord, by now there will be a stink!" (11:39).[47] It would be easy to consign her objection to mere descriptive

---

44. Sometimes this preparation would take place in the courtyard of the family's tomb.

45. See Hanger, *Sensing Salvation*, 123. Magness ("Ossuaries") notes that families who couldn't afford a tomb would bury the body in a grave.

46. Klink (*John*, 509) notes that this would protect against impurity. See also Hachlili, *Jewish Funerary Customs*, 447.

47. Kurek-Chomycz ("Fragrance of Her Perfume," 341) notes that this is the only explicit mention of a negative smell in the entire New Testament. This same word

detail. But this actually provides a window into how Martha views Lazarus. The anticipated stench highlights death's absolute finality, its irreversible permanence. As Lazarus's body has begun the decomposition process, Martha is walking through Howes's transition, grieving the loss of her brother as she witnesses his living presence decompose into beloved ancestral memory.

Now, imagine and trace with your nose what *might* follow Jesus's command to open the tomb. I am tentative here because there is no mention of an actual stench, only a predicted one. This has led to mixed opinions about its presence.[48] I will leave you to determine what you think, but the following takes the liberty to presume that the four-days-expired Lazarus emits an odor that is hard to handle. The collection of mourners who heft away the stone are close enough to inhale any stench that wafts and curls out from the tomb. And then, prompting further delay, Jesus lifts his eyes to heaven and prays to the Father.

Jesus finally calls Lazarus out of the tomb, and John narrates that *the dead man comes out*! This makes a lasting impression on those present. After all, this event is the final catalyst for Jesus's arrest, and it also leads many to become disciples of Jesus (11:45). For anyone inhaling the stink of death *and* witnessing the sights and sounds of life, this reversal would create an astonishing olfactive memory: Who has ever witnessed life emerge from the stench of death?

From Stench to Fragrance

Not long after the raising of Lazarus, in the very next chapter, John explicitly mentions smell again, but this time it's a pleasing fragrance (John 12:1–8). This scent connects back to Lazarus's stench of death. John narrates the links: Jesus returns to Bethany and attends a dinner given in his honor. Since Martha is serving the meal

---

appears in the Greek text of Exod. 8:10 (8:14 in English Bibles) to reference the stink of rotting frogs.

48. Wright (*Resurrection*, 443) doesn't think that there would be any smell, given Jesus's answered prayer for Lazarus to remain "uncorrupt." Lincoln ("Lazarus Story," 217–18n18) says that Wright reads too much into the story. Indeed, if Lazarus is narrated as dead, then four days is a long time, and I'm not sure why there wouldn't be a smell.

and Lazarus is reclining at the table, this is probably to celebrate what Jesus has done for Lazarus and the Bethany family. At the center of the action is Mary, who takes a pint of nard and pours it out on Jesus's feet, wiping them with her hair.[49] At this point fragrance is merely implied, similar to the Synoptic versions.[50] But then John explicitly narrates, "And the house was filled with the *fragrance* of the perfume" (12:3; cf. 11:2).

As in Matthew and Mark, disciples object to Mary's act—here it's Judas who disingenuously supposes that the perfume could have benefited the poor. Jesus is quick to defend Mary, and in so doing he interprets her gesture, saying, "Leave her alone. It was intended that she should save this perfume for the day of my burial" (12:7). Mary's fragrant act is aligned with Jesus's death.

Let's go back and reflect on how smells interact with themes of life and death. Jesus has just summoned life out of the stench of death. Lazarus's new life sets in motion the events leading to Jesus's death. Mary now punctuates this coming event by anointing Jesus for his burial. I suppose one could argue that the fragrance of her perfume also qualifies as "the smell of death," if not for the fact that it is a death that actually will germinate into life for the world. As New Testament scholar Marianne Meye Thompson states, "What brings life to Lazarus brings death to Jesus—but what brings death to Jesus brings life to the world."[51]

Some think that Mary's preburial anointing suggests royal, messianic connotations.[52] Another possible resonance is that this fragrance "filling the house" is analogous to God's glory "filling the house" when the temple and tabernacle are consecrated (Exod. 40:34–40; 1 Kings 8:10–11).[53] I think it's possible that each of these layers of meaning is in play for some of the earliest readers. But at the most basic level of this gesture, Mary is a disciple humbly expressing her

---

49. Many modern perfumes come in 3.4-ounce bottles, so that's four or five bottles' worth of a very aromatic perfume.

50. Nard, like incense, would naturally make one think of its aroma.

51. Thompson, "Raising of Lazarus," 237.

52. Klink (*John*, 525) suggests that the perfume scent was "symptomatic of the office of the king in both the OT and pagan contexts." Keener (*John*, 2:865) also observes that Mary could have intended this as a royal anointing.

53. Keener, *John*, 2:864.

gratitude and devotion to Jesus. In her desire to honor him, she brings out the most valuable asset she owns—this pure, fragrant nard. Anointing Jesus with abundant perfume is her way of conveying her heart, which is spilling over with fragrant affection.[54] In essence, Mary's perfume is a wordless, scented articulation of her love for Jesus. She has recognized Jesus to be exactly who he claims to be: the resurrection and the life. It's a response that turns out to be a preburial anointing.

We are not told how anyone beyond Judas responds to Mary's act. Her act is surprising because of its scent but also because of its tactile quality (which I will say more about in the next chapter). As we've said about the Synoptic accounts, it's possible that this fragrance connects with the onlookers' astonishment. Would future encounters with spikenard remind them of this anointing? Is it a mere coincidence that in the very next chapter Jesus washes his own disciples' feet? Is he mindful of what Mary has just done for him? Finally, how long does the scent of this perfume remain on Jesus's body? It happens less than a week before Jesus's death. What kind of preburial scents travel with him into the final traumatic events of his life?

Another Fragrant Anointing

It's hard to top what Mary offers Jesus in her fragrant, possibly royal, preburial gesture of affection. But when we arrive at Jesus's actual burial, we encounter another aromatic offering. After Jesus's body is removed from the cross, Joseph of Arimathea procures it from Pilate (John 19:38). Accompanying him is Nicodemus, who has brought seventy-five pounds of myrrh and aloes (19:39). Here we are back to implicit scents, but most interpreters notice the superabundance of these spices mirroring the volume of Mary's perfume. The men follow Jewish burial customs and apply the aromatics to Jesus's body as they wrap it in strips of linen (19:40). This is how someone might bestow high honors on a king.[55] This implicit fragrance is paired with the scents of the garden setting of the tomb, mentioned

---

54. Cosgrove ("Woman's Unbound Hair," 688) views this as an act of her devotion and affection.
55. Klink, *John*, 818.

at Jesus's burial (19:41) and then wafting in again when Mary Magdalene mistakes the risen Jesus for the gardener (20:15). Fragrance, once again, hovers around the themes of death and life.

Smell for the Earliest Readers

As with the other senses we've explored, the earliest readers had the advantage of an embodied resonance with the smells narrated within the Gospels. In contrast to our modern, Western, "unscented" spaces, the earliest readers would have known the smells of ancient households, crowded streets, festival settings, and funerary processions, having inhaled the scents swirling around in the villages and cities of the ancient world. They would have known what incense smells like in the context of devotion to God. They would have been close enough in cultural context to have smelled the types of foods present at a banquet. If you asked them, "Can you imagine the stench of Lazarus's tomb?" they could have answered, "Yes!" It was that much easier to step inside the Gospel narratives with an embodied knowledge of these finer details.

For the earliest readers there would have been an embodied awareness of how smell attached to social class, economic standing, and gender. This gave them immediate resonance with the narrative. On the downside, since these were the waters in which they swam, they possibly would have resonated *less* with the people groups from which they were excluded. This is why it would have been so important for ancient female readers to see Mary affirmed when she stopped cooking and sat in the posture of disciple at Jesus's feet. This is why it was critical for disciples to understand that an abundance of perfume poured on Jesus's feet is *not* a waste but was actually something to affirm and remember.

Reflections on Smell for Modern Readers

I've spent much of this chapter making the case that smell is potent despite its silence and invisibility. Are you a believer yet? Do you believe that smell matters to how we engage the Gospels? It's true, the presence of smell is mostly hidden within narrative worlds, leaving us to imagine what a setting *might* have smelled like. I suspect that for some, grappling with implied smells in the Gospel narratives does little more than describe the text more fully. In other words, many will still consider smell more decorative than critical to our understanding of the Gospels.

But this is not true of everyone. Helen Keller reminds us of the importance of aroma. During her lifetime she was often judged as having lesser intelligence because of her lack of sight and hearing.[56] Her response to these critics demonstrates otherwise, as she beautifully articulates a world governed by taste, touch, and smell. About smell specifically, she once famously wrote, "Smell is a potent wizard that transports us across thousands of miles and all the years we have lived."[57] Keller brings out aspects of this multisensory life that many who rely mostly on sight and hearing would never pick up on. All of us are better for her contribution.

Why does smell matter to our study of the Gospels? There are two reasons. At the risk of sounding overly simplistic, contemplating smell reminds us of the holistic beauty and goodness of God's big world. It can heighten our response of praise for a God who cared enough to fill in every last detail of our experience of this world. And it's remarkable that scents have been designed to infiltrate our bodies to the point that they influence our memories, our emotions, our affections, and our actions.

How can smell help us engage with the Gospels and Jesus today in our setting? After all, most of us read Scripture using our eyes, or we listen to it with our ears, or we talk about it with our mouths, as we flip through the pages of a Bible with our fingers. I'd guess that all of this tends to occur in settings that are either fragrance-free or are fragrance-friendly-to-us environments. Perhaps a starting point is to consider how smell figures into devotion to God.

What do certain smells remind you of? What scents unearth nostalgia, and which ones trigger sadness, anger, or anxiety? Which ones make you want to dance, celebrate, and express gratitude to

56. Keller writes about this in *The World I Live In*.
57. Keller, *The World I Live In*, 79.

God? Now, can you dig deeper? Why do these smells prompt such emotions? Do they tie back to a core memory? What about that memory brings up such deeply held feelings about yourself, or God, or others?

Can a certain smell bring you into conversation with God? How might a particular scent in your life resonate with something you read about in the Gospels? Do the smells associated with devotion to God prompt you to create your own patterns of scent as you consider your own life with him? If you have not yet considered the role of smell in your life as a reader of the Gospels, I invite you to simply pay attention, reflect, and relish in the goodness of the fragrant corner of the earth you occupy.

THE PLEASANT SCENTS
OF SALVATION

1. Spend a considerable length of time simply noticing the various aromas that exist in your world. Catalog some of these smells: Where do they come from? When do you experience these smells the most and with whom? How do they make you feel? After reflecting on these aromas over a length of time, can you turn your awareness of smell into an opportunity to praise God for this good and fragrant world? Spend some time talking to him about it, whether verbally or in writing.

2. Find a setting that gives off a pleasant scent and spend some time in it with awareness of God's presence. This could be a natural set of smells, such as a grove of trees or the beach. This could be everyday scents, like brewing coffee or baking bread. Or this could be a manufactured smell, such as a favorite scented candle. Spend some time talking with God about it. What are you grateful for? What do you notice about this good world he has created? What questions do you have? Enjoy the air and breathe deeply.

3. Spend some time reading and reflecting on *one* of the Gospel's anointing scenes: Matthew 26:6–13; Mark 14:3–9; Luke 7:36–50;

John 12:1–8. Reflecting on the fragrance of the scene, consider the extravagance of the woman's anointing. How might this encourage you in your own expression of devotion to Jesus?

7

Just a Touch of Love

Jesus and the Potency of Touch

Back in 2014, a happy meetup between some royals sparked a bit of a dustup in the British tabloids. During a three-day visit to New York, United Kingdom royals Prince William and his wife, Princess Catherine (Kate Middleton), took in an evening of basketball played between the Cleveland Cavaliers and the Brooklyn Nets. Afterward, they connected with United States "royal" LeBron James, popularly dubbed "King James" (so not *exactly* a royal). After the game there was a photo opportunity for William, Kate, and LeBron together, standing side by side. Perhaps unremarkable to American sensibilities, LeBron put his arm around Kate as they posed for the pic. Oops! What we in the United States might consider to be a show of friendly affection was interpreted by the Brits to be a breach of etiquette, since to touch a royal without being touched first is considered a faux pas. Now if Kate was bothered by this, it was not obvious. But it's moments like these that remind us of the rules that various cultures assign to sensory interactions involving touch.

For anyone reluctant to believe that they live in a culture with rules about touch, here is another example. When the COVID-19 pandemic hit, we came face-to-face with our culture's tactile rules as we experienced their complete upheaval. Our former rules around touch were broadly construed to suggest that proximity and touch are an expression of care for someone else. But in the earliest days of lockdown this type of casual touch was flipped. Suddenly, touch had become potentially dangerous for someone's health. We had to express love *without* touch. This was hard! This extended season generated the term "social distance," where suddenly the greatest kindness you could extend to someone was to carve a wide path around them as you passed on the sidewalk. In a prepandemic world this action might have been considered rude, as if you were avoiding someone because they smelled bad or carried some type of social contagion. Many of us were conditioned to communicate love and kindness with a hug or a handshake. To suddenly be without these practices took its toll, affecting individuals, families, and the broader society at large.[1]

We are embarking on our exploration of how touch operates in the Gospels—our final sensory capacity of this book. As with smell, we tend to overlook the presence of touch because it is part of the fabric of our lives, integral to our comings and goings. It's often when we experience disruption to our rules around touch that we stop to reflect on how we relate to it.

As with the other senses, the dynamics of touch vary depending on the setting. For example, we can address how touch operates in larger social and cultural settings, such as the pandemic example. We can also address touch in smaller settings, like family systems. In my extended family, for example, we commonly greet one another with a kiss and a hug. However, I'm not likely to plant a kiss on the cheek of my university colleagues when I reunite with them after a long summer apart. Why? Because tactile rules are different in a place of employment. Finally, we can address touch on an individual level. Within my immediate family I have one child who feels loved when I provide a hearty back scratch, while I have another who is touch

---

1. See, for example, Mohr, Kirsch, and Fotopoulou, "Social Touch Deprivation." Their study surveyed 1,746 people about their experience with pandemic-related social distance and touch restrictions. Ultimately, their research revealed the positive effects of social and intimate touch, with touch deprivation leading to greater levels of anxiety and loneliness.

averse and would squirm at such contact, preferring that I express affection with words and actions.

As we seek further understanding of how touch operates in various settings, it will help to explore the characteristics of touch. The following will address both its anatomy and potency.

The Complexities of Touch

The sense of touch is multifaceted. It facilitates a variety of sensations we experience every day, such as heat and cold, or pleasure and pain. Sometimes we experience more than one of these responses at the same time, such as heat that produces pain, or cold that is soothing on a sweltering day. The complexity of touch intensifies as we consider how touch is valued. On the one hand, Aristotle ranks touch at the bottom of his five-sense hierarchy, but on the other hand, he considers it a crucial sense for sustaining life. How can these two valuations hold together?

The Anatomy of Touch

The anatomy of touch helps to explain how touch can be both extremely important and yet ranked so low. First, touch is the most directly experienced physical sense.[2] Skin is the organ of touch, which necessitates close interaction.[3] Contrasting this, sight (along with hearing and smell) operates at more of a distance. Consider Walter Ong's observation about the limitations of a sense like sight: "Sight reveals only surfaces. It can never get to an interior as an interior, but must always treat it as somehow an exterior."[4] Touch necessitates up-close contact.

2. Taste also involves touch, although Aristotle (*On the Soul* 2.422a15) observes that its direct connection point is limited to the touch of the tongue, while touch is mediated through the larger medium of skin. (As a side note, this reminds us of the overlapping nature of the senses—taste with touch, taste with smell, and even smell with touch, if you consider the "touch" of particles to the nasal cavity.)

3. Aristotle (*On the Soul* 2.423b17–18) discusses its direct nature since "we perceive tangible things not by a medium, but at the same time as the medium."

4. Ong, *Presence of the Word*, 74. Of course, in recent years sight *has* traveled beneath surfaces with x-ray and MRI technology (though in operation even this interior quality of sight differs from the invasive, intimate quality of touch of these inner parts).

Skin is also the largest organ of the human body, which makes touch a very commonly engaged sense perception, facilitating a diversity of interactions. Social and cultural science researcher Isobel Sigley suggests that touch is the sense we think about the least because "we strain to hear, we focus our eyes, refine our taste buds, deeply inhale a pleasant smell, and yet, when we touch, it is more often a means to an end."[5] We frequently engage touch unconsciously because it is so entrenched in our day-to-day action. Constance Classen adds that touch "lies at the heart of our experience of ourselves yet it often remains unspoken."[6] Perhaps this is why touch tends to be overlooked: it's simply so common and ingrained.

This is also why Aristotle demotes it to such a low rank; he considers it the basest, most foundational sense. It's the most common element for maintaining life, including animal and plant life.[7] Susan Stewart observes that while other senses are involved with our "well-being," touch is needed for "being."[8] Touch is one of the earliest experienced senses; a fetus will respond to touch before eyes and ears are formed.[9] Infants require nurturing touch for survival, and lack of touch can have negative effects on brain development. Neglect invests a sense of low self-worth into a child.[10]

Herein lies the complexity of touch. Aristotle considers touch foundational for sustaining life, but its commonality is what leads him to rank it so low. Its ordinary quality also makes it less a candidate for elevation to the level of philosophical reflection. Another complicating factor is how touch—like the other four senses—attaches to social and economic class, gender, and morality. These dynamics hold touch in place at the bottom of the rankings, preventing it from being cultivated in sophistication beyond its daily operations.

5. Sigley, "It Has Touched Us All," 2.

6. Classen, *Deepest Sense*, xi. Elsewhere Classen ("Fingertips," 2) observes how we take touch for granted as a "medium for the production of meaningful acts, rather than meaningful in itself."

7. Aristotle, *On the Soul* 2.413b. He includes taste and its nutritive operations as part of what touch accomplishes to maintain life.

8. Stewart, "Remembering the Senses," 61.

9. Montagu, *Touching*, 3.

10. Arel, *Affect Theory*, 132. See also Hanger, "Role of Touch," 45.

Touch Is Powerful

One contributing factor to the potency of touch is its proximity. Reaching out and touching someone on the shoulder requires that we get right up close to them. This proximity is heightened by its reciprocity: touch affects the one who initiates it and the one who receives it. Touch involves "lived experiences" compared with "intellectual abstractions."[11] For those conditioned within environments that prioritize detached, visually dominant patterns of living, touch can be perceived as "the most direct invasion."[12]

When you add this proximity to the ubiquitous experience of touch, it compounds its potency. Touch facilitates such a wide variety of actions that it is intricately involved in our most meaningful—and often our most traumatic—interactions. Touch can help to nurture and express love, but it also can be used to facilitate negative physical contact, including intimidation, manipulation, and violence.

Finally, touch is potent in its ability both to extend into symbolic importance and to effect change in relationships. Consider the significance of a handshake between enemies. This physical gesture acts as a symbol of unity while simultaneously injecting greater importance into the embodied interaction. A simple handshake can move enemies toward reconciliation.

Modern and Ancient Tactile Contexts

It is perhaps *because* of the power of touch that we have so many rules structuring its expression. Ruth Finnegan talks about how all people groups have rules around who can touch whom, for what purpose(s), and in what way(s). These rules are often unspoken, but they exist nonetheless.[13]

Modern and ancient tactile rules tend to revolve around people's ultimate thriving, protecting from harm and fostering nurturing, empathic connections. When the global pandemic upended our rules around touch, making it dangerous, we learned that we are disposed to believe that nurturing touch can convey empathy. However, tactile

11. Howes and Classen, *Ways of Sensing*, 7.
12. Finnegan, "Tactile Communication," 18.
13. Finnegan, "Tactile Communication," 18.

rules—in modern and ancient contexts—do not always follow this pattern of nurture and protection. This becomes evident when we return to previous observations about how the senses are linked to social and economic class and to gender.[14] Jerry Toner points out how ancient elite classes often associated lower classes with the more "unpleasant sensations" of touch, while they enjoyed the "luxury" of limited tactile contact in spacious living quarters.[15] More jarring are the examples of tactile standards that exacted violence and injustice on underprivileged classes. Slaves were distinguishable from elites by the marks they bore on their skin from torture and, frequently, branding.[16] As property, slaves often served "to enhance the sensual pleasures of his or her owners, either through the work they did or as sexual objects."[17] Women were connected to rules around touch that dictated their daily freedoms and constraints. Higher value was placed on modest women, which meant staying home, with hair bound and heads covered. To be out in public could expose them to "possible moral contagion." Economics here combines with gender, since poorer women who had to work—in urban *and* rural settings—were out and about in the cities and markets, which in turn affected their perceived modesty.[18]

Tactile Contact in Scripture

When we examine touch throughout the Gospels, we immediately confront rules about touch in a Jewish context, particularly regarding questions about ritual purity. There are many times when Jesus encounters friction with the religious leaders because he touches (or is touched by) someone deemed ritually impure, breaking protocol and crossing tactile boundaries.

Helpful to this conversation is the reminder that the purity system was initiated out of compassion. Writing about this landscape, New Testament scholar Matthew Thiessen states that the purity system "was a protective and benevolent system intended to preserve God's

14. Sigley ("It Has Touched Us All") discusses how the pandemic diversely affected touch among different economic classes, ethnicities, and minority groups.
15. Toner, "Sensing the Ancient Past," 6.
16. Toner, "Sensing the Ancient Past," 6.
17. Aldrete, "Urban Sensations," 61.
18. Aldrete, "Urban Sensations," 63.

presence among his people."[19] God is loving and merciful, yes, but his holy presence is so powerful that coming near him in the wrong way could be hazardous, even deadly. (This is not unlike the sun—a good, powerful life force, but dangerous if you draw too close.) We see examples of such consequences, such as the deaths of the priests Nadab and Abihu (Lev. 10:1–7) and Uzzah (2 Sam. 6:6–11) because they approach God's presence wrongly. The moral and ritual purity standards in Leviticus are for Israel's protection and to preserve God's presence among his people. This reminds us also of God's holiness and the potency of his glory.

Jesus is often interpreted as coming on the scene to oppose this ritual purity system. To the contrary, Thiessen contends (convincingly, in my view), what Jesus is opposing is the *source* of ritual impurity rather than the system itself.[20] Remember how as the "Word become flesh" (John 1:14), Jesus is described as the "Holy One of God" (Mark 1:24). In his holiness, Jesus is a "contagious power" that "overwhelms the forces of impurity."[21] When he heals a man of leprosy, he is not opposing the purity system so much as he is eradicating the "forces of death" that created the impurity in the first place.

Hence, the Jewish purity system is a good thing in the life of God's people, but its "ritual detergents" are limited in their capacity to remove impurities.[22] Thiessen observes how the purity system could remove "the lingering effects" of the condition that made someone impure, but it could not (and was never intended to) remove the physical condition causing the impurity.[23] Jesus comes along and is able to eradicate the forces of death: both their lingering effects *and* the physical condition causing them. Thiessen summarizes, "God [has] introduced something *new* into the world to deal with the sources of these impurities: Jesus."[24]

19. Thiessen, *Jesus*, 11.
20. Thiessen, *Jesus*, 6.
21. Thiessen, *Jesus*, 6.
22. Thiessen, *Jesus*, 19.
23. Thiessen, *Jesus*, 19.
24. Thiessen, *Jesus*, 179. He nuances any urge toward supersessionist thinking, clarifying how the early church understood that "in Messiah Jesus, the old cosmos was being superseded by a new creation in which Satan and his demons, death, and sin . . . would no longer exist" (183).

As we delve into the tactile Synoptic passages, the foregoing conversation about purity and impurity will be immediately relevant. When Jesus engages others using touch, often it causes quite a stir. This largely has to do with how Jesus disrupts these established tactile purity standards.

Touch in the Synoptics

Jesus ministers to people in a variety of tactile and nontactile modalities.[25] Craig Evans reports that Jesus reaches out his hand or receives tactile contact about nine times in Matthew, eleven times in Mark, and thirteen times in Luke.[26] Of Jesus's healings by touch, Joel Green notes that "one looks in vain for direct OT precedence for the laying on of hands as a component of the process of miraculous healing."[27] He goes on to wonder if Jesus's laying on of hands is an "extension of God's own hand to act in creation and redemption."[28]

We will be tracing two major threads as we peruse these Synoptic narratives. First, we will address how Jesus disrupts rules around touch related to purity standards, social norms, economics, and gender. Second, we will observe how touch operates to convey a level of dignity and compassion that cannot be communicated using any other sensory capacity. In other words, the touch of Jesus conveys the message "I *see* you and I *care* about you" far better than only saying such words could accomplish.

The Healing Touch of Jesus

Let's begin by exploring how Jesus heals Peter's mother-in-law. Matthew reports that Jesus "touched her hand" (8:15), while Mark

25. Encountering the Capernaum centurion, Jesus heals his servant without even entering his household.

26. Evans, *Matthew*, 191. See also Wahlen, "Healing." Wahlen includes a table displaying modes of healing, by word and/or touch (364).

27. Green, *Luke*, 226. The one exception, he says, is a Qumran text in which Abram recalls being asked to lay his hand on the king of Egypt to pray for healing (1QGenesis Apocryphon 20:21–22). Although Stein (*Mark*, 266) comments that Jairus's request for Jesus to lay hands on his daughter would represent a common way to pass on a blessing or bring about a healing.

28. Green, *Luke*, 226.

says that he "took her hand" (1:31).[29] As he helps her up, the fever leaves her body. That same evening Jesus welcomes many at the doorstep of Peter's home. He heals those suffering from various diseases by "laying his hands on each one" (Luke 4:40). Finally, when Jesus restores sight, there are two separate occasions when he encounters blind men. Both times he touches their eyes (Matt. 9:29; 20:34). The latter of these accounts adds that Jesus's touch is accompanied by compassion. This sampling reveals how common it is for Jesus to engage others up close as he heals them.

All three Synoptics include the time a man with leprosy approaches Jesus and seeks healing (Matt. 8:1–4; Mark 1:40–45; Luke 5:12–16). Recent clarifications have been offered to describe what constitutes "leprosy" in the Bible.[30] The term probably encompasses a variety of mild-to-severe skin diseases that could produce sores, lesions, and disfigurations.[31] Regardless of the severity of disease that branded someone a "leper," such a condition was deeply debilitating, viewed as "the equivalent of death."[32] Often considered to be brought on as punishment for sin (Num. 12:1–15; 2 Kings 5:25–27; 2 Chron. 26:16–21),[33] leprosy is identified by Joel Green as a "social disease." It would have rendered someone ritually impure, and it would have required their separation from the community (Lev. 13).[34] It's probably important to clarify that residing in ritual impurity is not considered sinful according to priestly standards—after all, ritual and moral impurities were not brought on the same way.[35] However, the

29. You might remember that we looked at this scene when discussing smell.

30. You may have been taught, as I was, that leprosy is a severe skin condition causing the loss of feeling within one's body, leading eventually to the loss of various extremities, like a finger or a foot. Scholars now clarify that this condition—today called Hansen's disease—probably was not the same version of leprosy (Greek: *lepra*) referred to in the Bible. Thiessen (*Jesus*, 44) clarifies that the Greek term *lepra* is *ṣāra'at* in Hebrew and does not correspond to what we think of as leprosy.

31. Thiessen, *Jesus*, 43–68; Chen, *Luke*, 73–74; Stein, *Mark*, 105.

32. Thiessen (*Jesus*, 59) cites Rabbi Yohanan as referencing Naaman in 2 Kings 5. The king of Israel also equates a cure of leprosy with bringing someone back to life (2 Kings 5:7).

33. Stein, *Mark*, 105.

34. Green, *Luke*, 236.

35. Thiessen (*Jesus*, 9–20) is extremely helpful in clarifying the difference between ritual and moral impurity. Ritual impurity was inevitable, due to natural substances,

degree to which these categories were conflated is unclear; if people believed leprosy was judgment for sin, then it could dictate how they treated the afflicted.

This makes Jesus's interaction with the man significant since Jesus heals him by the touch of his hand. Ancient readers would immediately recognize this contact as rendering Jesus ritually impure, not to mention exposing him to the disease. But notice: when Jesus says "Be clean!" the leprosy immediately leaves the man and *he is cleansed* (Mark 1:41–42). Rather than Jesus becoming *un*clean, Jesus cleanses the man.[36] Jesus then sends him to the priest to offer the appropriate sacrifices for his cleansing, "as a testimony to them" (1:44). This would effectively restore the man to his community.[37]

Jesus's purification of this man is remarkable for a couple of reasons. First, as Thiessen points out, priests were only ever equipped to diagnose *lepra*, not to cure it: "Jesus's purification of the man is an astounding deed of power that Leviticus never envisages the priests performing."[38] With the touch of his hand, Jesus destroys the condition that created the impurity in the first place! This falls in line with the kinds of acts that signify God's coming kingdom (Matt. 11:5; Luke 7:22).[39]

Second, notice the way the Gospel writers portray the compassionate tenor of this interaction. When the man approaches Jesus, he memorably states, "If you are willing, you can make me clean" (Matt. 8:2; Mark 1:40; Luke 5:12). Matthew and Luke simply report Jesus as being willing: "I am willing. Be clean!" Depending on the translation, Mark additionally reports a willingness sparked by indignation (NIV), pity (NRSVue, ESV), or compassion (NASB).[40] We won't get into the text-critical conversation around which term is represented in the earliest manuscripts, but it's worth considering what Jesus might

---

could be bathed away, and was not considered sinful. Moral impurity was avoidable, the result of one's sinful actions, and required atonement.

36. Stein, *Mark*, 106.

37. Green (*Luke*, 237) observes how Jesus's touch was deliberate: it was contact that violated the law, but it also conveyed acceptance back into the community.

38. Thiessen (*Jesus*, 62–63) contrasts priestly and prophetic roles as they relate to *lepra*, pointing out that we *do* see leprosy cured by prophets, such as Miriam with Moses (Num. 12) and Naaman with Elisha (2 Kings 5).

39. Stein, *Mark*, 106.

40. Thiessen, *Jesus*, 54–65.

be indignant about. Thiessen believes that Jesus's anger is over the man questioning whether or not Jesus *wants* to purify him. In other words, the man believes in Jesus's ability to heal but wonders about his *willingness* to do so. This reading aligns with the translations citing Jesus's compassion. Either way, it communicates that *of course* Jesus wants the man to be cleansed. He *is* willing. He wants the man to be restored to full health and participation in his community.

Let's look more closely at the touch of Jesus. Is Jesus's tactile contact required to cleanse this man? Not necessarily. Think about the *effect* of Jesus touching an "untouchable" man who probably has grown accustomed in his leprosy to *not* being touched. He is considered to be a contagion to his community. However long he has been afflicted with *lepra* dictates the kinds of embodied rhythms of isolation he adheres to, day in and day out. On top of the actual cleansing, Jesus's healing touch cannot avoid *also* serving as a gesture that conveys a level of compassion for this man. In other words, there is something inherently loving in Jesus's touch.

Thus, Jesus laying healing hands on someone is quite potent. Now, what happens when the reverse occurs? In the next section, we will explore the times when Jesus is the *recipient* of touch.

Jesus Receives Touch

As you peruse the Gospels, you will see interactions that portray Jesus as carrying healing power within himself, where merely touching him (or his clothing) seems to have some kind of magical curative effect.

Shortly after Jesus feeds the multitude and walks on the sea, he lands at Gennesaret, and Matthew reports people bringing their sick to him. They "begged him to let the sick just *touch* the edge of his cloak, and *all who touched it were healed*" (14:36). Perhaps they do this because word has gotten out that this worked before (Matt. 9), or maybe the crowd is so large that they are worried about getting an audience with Jesus. If just a touch of his garment would work, they would try it.[41] One thing that this suggests is the magnitude of Jesus's power available

41. Osborne, *Matthew*, 581. He also notes that the "edge" of Jesus's "cloak" could be referring to the four corners at the bottom of the robe, where the "tassels" would be (Num. 15:38–41; Deut. 22:12).

to anyone who would draw near enough to touch him, even if only his clothing. Once again, Jesus seems unconcerned about making physical contact with those who might render him ritually impure.

Another time, as a large crowd assembles to hear Jesus teach, Luke reports that "the people all tried to touch him, because power was coming from him and healing them all" (6:19). Power is *going out* from Jesus? Remarkable! Again, the understanding of healing locates the power of God as resident *in* Jesus, potent enough to restore all who are close enough to touch his garments.[42]

Probably the most well-known instance of someone initiating tactile contact with Jesus is when the woman with the hemorrhage jostles her way through a crowd to grasp Jesus's cloak. Here, again, power goes out from Jesus, and seemingly without Jesus even being in control of it! Luke highlights this in Jesus's response: "Someone touched me; I know that power has gone out from me" (8:46). This woman's story is worth rewinding a bit in order to understand the magnitude of this interaction.

Her predicament is dire. She appears to be suffering from some kind of uncontrolled menstrual bleeding. In the ancient context this is more alarming than what we might experience today. (Hear me out, ladies, because yes, twelve years in any era is a long time to be dealing with such matters.) Think about the disheartening lack of available technology in her context: there were no pills she could take, no ultrasound diagnostics, and no surgical procedures to alleviate her suffering. Any resources that *did* exist she exhausted, spending all her money only to make things worse (Mark 5:26).

Ancient readers would have immediately observed the impropriety of the woman approaching Jesus while in a state of ritual impurity. Her prolonged abnormal bleeding would render everything she comes into contact with ritually impure. Now, this doesn't necessarily mean that she is required to remain in complete seclusion.[43] It also doesn't mean that she is in sin for touching a ritually pure person. Thiessen reminds us that ritual impurity—or passing it on—is not a sin unless

---

42. Carroll, *Luke*, 147.

43. Thiessen (*Jesus*, 85–86) disagrees with scholars who suggest that by mingling with a crowd she is being negligent toward others. He also disagrees with suggestions that Jesus's disregard of her touch indicates his desire to overturn the purity system.

it is brought into sacred space.[44] And, he suggests, we are unsure how strictly these purity practices are followed in her context. Is quarantine expected? Not necessarily. Note how there is precedent for proper washing that ensures that impurities would not pass to others (Lev. 15:11). The one thing that *is* certain is that for over a decade she would not have been permitted to participate with her community in regular rhythms of devotion in sacred spaces like the temple. This alone might send her into a difficult level of social isolation.

There are further implications of her state of ritual impurity. According to modern definitions of disability, New Testament scholar Louise Gosbell contends that we should read this woman as someone with a disability in her first-century Greco-Roman context.[45] This is because for a woman in the ancient world, any illness inhibiting her ability to fulfill her domestic vocation would have debilitating effects on her daily life.[46] If this woman's twelve years of bleeding spans across any of her childbearing years, this would be catastrophic. Her state of impurity would mean abstinence from sexual relations with her husband, if she already had one.[47] But even *with* a husband her condition likely renders her infertile, which in turn puts her under the looming threat of divorce. An even worse scenario is if she contracted this disease *before* marriage and children, which would prevent her from acquiring both. By the time she encounters Jesus, she's whittled away her most fertile years trying to find relief from this debilitating illness.[48] In contrast to the financial outlets available to many women today to offset these limitations, she lacks options.

Can you feel her desperation? No doubt she has heard about this miracle worker, so she musters up just enough faith to pep talk herself into Jesus's presence (Mark 5:28). As she reaches out and grasps

44. Thiessen, *Jesus*, 87.
45. Gosbell, "Woman with the 'Flow of Blood,'" 23. Current definitions of disability involve physical and social impairments that limit one's activity.
46. Gosbell, "Woman with the 'Flow of Blood,'" 24.
47. In Mark's telling, she spent all *her* money (5:26), which suggests that she is alone, especially when contrasted with Jairus's daughter, whose father was her advocate.
48. Carroll (*Luke*, 199) suggests that Luke's rendering (8:43) could read that she has been subject to bleeding either "for twelve years" (the way we tend to read it) or "from [the age of] twelve years [onward]." The latter reading would mean that she had suffered her entire adult life to that point.

the edge of Jesus's cloak, she feels and knows it immediately: she is healed! I love the parallel that Thiessen highlights: just as the woman has had this "uncontrolled discharge of blood leaking from her body," notice that Mark presents Jesus healing her by an "uncontrolled discharge [of power] from his own body."[49] Extraordinary! Her touch of Jesus's garment, initially perceived to be contaminating, turns out to have called forth Jesus's healing power.

From here, Jesus demands to know who touched his clothes. He could have left it alone, but he doesn't. This, I think, displays Jesus's compassion: he wants holistic restoration for her. She comes trembling to his feet and tells him the whole truth, and Jesus responds by addressing her as "daughter," proclaiming that her faith has healed her (Mark 5:33–34). This is such an honoring way to lift her up in the eyes of her community. Giving her a platform to share what he has done completes her restoration. She is healed and no longer ritually impure. Not only does she know it, but now, so does everyone else.

To this point we have explored the power dwelling in Jesus as he both reaches out to touch and is touched by many people throughout the Gospels. Not only does he provide physical healing, but also we have noted how his touch brings about cleansing, eradicating the forces of death that create ritual impurity. We have also begun to see how his touch conveys a unique brand of compassion. It is to this quality of compassion that we turn next.

A Touch of Love

All three Synoptic Gospels briefly narrate the time when Jesus welcomes little ones—babies *and* children[50]—and places his hands on them. As Craig Evans suggests, in the ancient world there was a belief that touching a "holy man" could confer blessing.[51] Matthew adds that the people ask Jesus to pray for these children (19:13).

Jesus seems to be crossing some kind of boundary, because the disciples try to put the kibosh on the whole scene. They go so far

49. Thiessen, *Jesus*, 91.
50. Luke states that people were bringing their babies (Luke 18:15); Matthew and Mark broaden it to include children (Matt. 19:13; Mark 10:13).
51. Evans, *Matthew*, 343.

as to rebuke the children, or their parents, or both. They might be thinking that Jesus is too busy and important to stop and make time for children. In the ancient world, children were accorded low status,[52] possibly due to their high mortality rate. We are not entirely sure why the disciples aren't having it.

Jesus is quick to correct them, though, saying, "Let the little children come to me, and do not hinder them" (Matt. 19:14; Mark 10:14; Luke 18:16). Jesus is determined to bless them. Have you ever tried to imagine the loving tenor of these interactions? I find it easiest to lock eyes on the passages where Jesus is serious, delivering important teachings, playing theological chess with the academics of his day, casting out demons with the seriousness of a miracle-worker. Imagining *this* passage, I think that we can picture smiling eyes, peekaboo, shy-kid tears dissolving into giggles, gentle hands on heads, on shoulders, on arms. Parents must have also felt Jesus's compassion as he shared their joy over the littlest members of their families.

The kingdom, Jesus says, belongs to "such as these." *Such as these.* I would take that to mean that the kingdom is not only for children but for anyone who resembles these smallest little citizens among us. The kingdom is for those of low status, for those who are small in strength, for those who need an advocate, for those we overlook and disregard. Jesus welcomes all these with smiling eyes and a hand of blessing.

Let's look at one more tactile scene that we earlier inspected for its fragrance. Luke narrates about the time when a woman—a "sinner"— anoints Jesus with perfume (7:36–50). As she approaches Jesus, weeping, she is close enough for her tears to fall on his feet. As this happens, she wipes his feet with her hair, then kisses and pours perfume on them.

Right away we are clued in to this tactile faux pas, which is framed as judgment on Jesus by his host, who supposes, *If Jesus were really a prophet, he would know that a sinner is touching him.* The implication is, of course, that if Jesus knew she was a sinner, he wouldn't *let* her touch him. On the surface of things, her gesture *is* unusual. For one thing, it potentially comes across as erotic.[53] Diane Chen highlights the uncertain signals sent out by her let-down hair: Is this

52. Stein, *Mark*, 462.
53. Green, *Luke*, 311.

conveying sexual innuendo, or is she grieving?[54] Not only that, but engaging Jesus's feet, an unclean part of his body, highlights the humility of her gesture. Nothing about this exchange is "regular." But everything about it is welcomed by Jesus. He not only allows it, but he praises her for it. He tells a parable about forgiven debts, and she is the exemplar of the story, worthy of praise because she demonstrates her great, unabashed love for Jesus as she basks in the gratitude of her forgiven sin. She brings bold, honest, humble, heartfelt gratitude and love, literally poured out on Jesus. And touch is absolutely integral to this expression.

Trigger Warning: Violent Touch

We come to our last section before moving on to the Fourth Gospel. We have addressed the many compassionate tactile expressions between Jesus and others, but Jesus also suffers violence near the end of his time on earth. Let's look briefly at the tactile violence surrounding his trial.[55]

In particular I want to focus on the abuse that Jesus suffers at the hands of the guards before they lead him to be crucified. Matthew tells us that a whole company of soldiers surrounds him, strips him, and puts a scarlet robe on him, setting a crown of thorns on his head. They put a staff in his right hand, after which they mock him. They spit on him and then use the same staff to strike him repeatedly on his crowned head (27:27–30; cf. Mark 15:18–20). Luke mentions a mocking game they play, where they blindfold him, hit him, and tell him to prophesy who did it (22:63–65). Shortly after this, Jesus is changed back into his clothes and led to the cross.

What a horrible, degrading scene! It's difficult and unpleasant to imagine. Why conclude our review of the Synoptics on such a dissonant note? As we have been observing throughout this book, our sensory experiences have a way of becoming embedded deep into our brains and bodies. Bodies know. The Gospels remind us that Jesus knows, in his body, the violence of this life we live. For anyone whose

---

54. Chen, *Luke*, 104.
55. Stein (*Mark*, 711), like others, highlights the brevity of the description of Jesus's crucifixion, calling it "eloquently understated."

personal tactile rules have been shaped, dismantled, overturned, and traumatized by violent touch, I hope you know that Jesus shares this embodied knowledge too. Scenes like this remind us that the physical contact of touch in Jesus's life *and* death conveys a quality of compassion and solace that reminds us we are not alone. Let's look at how John articulates similar values.

Touch in the Fourth Gospel

Our preceding discussions have laid sufficient groundwork for us to get right into the Johannine tactile passages. The following scenes display similar themes to what we saw in the Synoptics, as we observe Jesus's touch overturning societal standards and conveying his compassion for people who might otherwise be undervalued.

Dignifying Contact

You might recall our discussion in chapter 4 of the interaction of sight with touch. All four Gospels tell about how Jesus creates sight for the blind by using the sense of touch. Here we witness the merging of the distant, higher-class sense of sight with the proximate, lower-class sense of touch. By doing so, Jesus is "speaking the language" of those who navigated through life largely by touch, engaging them in a familiar modality. This renders these interactions both intimate and humble.

In John 9, Jesus invites the man born blind to participate in his own healing: as Jesus applies the mud to his eyes, the man must go and wash it away before he can see. By this interactive sign, Jesus's touch literally raises the man up from the ground. How dignifying! The newly sighted man now has the option to leave his begging post and participate more fully in the life of his community.

John narrates that many are astonished—and resistant—to this sign. The formerly blind man is asked to rehearse this tactile interaction several times (9:10–11, 15, 26–27). People can't understand how this healing—and on the Sabbath, no less!—could be a work of God (9:16). Does its mode of healing—touch—serve at all as a hindrance to their belief? We can't be sure, but over the course of these interviews the man reaches a posture of belief in Jesus, while those in the religious establishment are declared blind for their unbelief (9:38–41).

What is clear is that Jesus values this societally overlooked man, the touch of his eyes effectively communicating to him, "You are here to me."[56] As Jesus creates sight from the dust of the ground, the man is invited to step into a new quality of life.

Fragrant Touch

Let's return to another familiar scene, in which Mary anoints Jesus with perfume for his burial (not to be confused with Luke's anointing).[57] In the previous chapter we inspected Mary's gesture for its fragrance. Here we focus on its tactile quality.[58] This is perhaps less noticed because touch is less explicit. We don't know if she directly touched Jesus's feet, since the passage simply says that "she poured [the pure nard] on Jesus's feet and wiped his feet with her hair" (John 12:3). Touch is largely mediated through her hair.

The clue that she is disrupting some kind of social protocol lies in Judas's protest. While he is objecting primarily to the expense of the perfume used on Jesus's feet, intrinsic to this act is the surprise generated from what comes *after* Mary pours the nard: she lets down her hair and uses it to wipe his feet. Similar to Luke's anointing, there is ambiguity about the propriety of this. For one thing, handling feet is typically the role of a servant.[59] This is further complicated by Mary's gender, and some might interpret her gesture as carrying sexual innuendo.[60] At the same time, this might be tempered by the ways touch is associated with her socially inferior gender, making her anointing less surprising than if a male disciple had initiated it. Apart from each of these dynamics, some might simply observe her

56. Arel, *Affect Theory*, 142.

57. As mentioned earlier, Luke seems to narrate a different anointing: in Luke 7:36–50 the unnamed woman is identified as a sinner who is in tears of gratitude for forgiveness, while in John 12:1–8 Jesus interprets Mary's gesture as a preburial anointing.

58. These insights are adapted from Hanger, "Role of Touch," 53–54.

59. Keener, *John*, 2:863; Thompson, *John*, 259; Klink, *John*, 525.

60. Keener (*John*, 2:864) observes that some might be suspicious of "too much cross-gender affection between nonrelatives," and in public, no less.

gesture as an expression of her grief or, more likely, her devotion and affection.[61] Surprised or not, Jesus goes on to defend her: "Leave her alone" (12:7). This is a preburial anointing, he says, adding further purpose to Mary's expression of love and devotion. Think about how Mary's touch mediates her love in a memorable way for Jesus also. Mutual touch is bidirectional. Mary applies a fragrance to express her heart, which Jesus receives into his own heart. His receptivity doubles back to confer dignity on Mary. This is a beautiful reciprocal exchange of love, mediated by touch (and fragrance). As Theodore of Mopsuestia states, "For it was as if the woman planned this so as to attach the fragrance of our Lord's flesh to her body. For she took care that she should always be with him: she did this in her love so that if she should come to be separated from him, by this she could suppose he was with her still."[62] I suspect that Jesus also takes this memory with him into his final embodied week of dramatic events, a fragrant reminder of others' love in the midst of the excruciating tactile violence he suffers.

Another Surprise Tactile Reversal

Mary's anointing lays the groundwork for a similar exchange of touch. Less than one week later, Jesus shares a final supper with his disciples, only this time he is the host. While the meal is in progress, Jesus gets up, takes off his outer clothing, and wraps a towel around his waist. Pouring water into a basin, he begins to wash his disciples' feet, drying them with the towel wrapped around him (John 13:4–5).

Peter's loud objection, "You shall never wash my feet," lets us know that Jesus is crossing a social boundary with this gesture (13:8a). A teacher would never wash the feet of a student. This is such a menial task, reserved for the lowest-ranked servants.[63] Sandaled feet on dusty roads were filthy and probably stinky. This makes

---

61. Cosgrove ("Woman's Unbound Hair") suggests, besides seduction, several other reasons why a woman might let down her hair—for example, to express gratitude, humility, reverence, freedom, naturalness, wildness, ferocity, mourning.

62. Theodore of Mopsuestia, *Commentarius in Evangelium Johannis Apostoli*, 233. The translation is from Coakley, "Anointing at Bethany," 252.

63. Keener (*John*, 2:904n49) notes that in some settings footwashing was considered improper even for a Jewish servant to carry out.

sense of why footwashing was considered to be such a lowly task. I would guess that intrinsic to Peter's protest is a tacit, visceral sense of "ick" fueling his conviction that Jesus is crossing a tactile boundary. *Jesus, you can't be serious. This is wrong.* Jesus's touch invades and overturns the social ranking system that Peter and the disciples are accustomed to.

This probably also lets us know that Peter doesn't fully understand *why* Jesus is washing his feet. John clues us in to the significance of this footwashing by setting it in the context of "the hour" of Jesus's departure and his love for the disciples "to the end."[64] Many will therefore link the footwashing to his death, interpreting it as a symbolic prefiguring of the cleansing and forgiveness of sins that the cross accomplishes.[65] Jesus affirms this by responding to Peter's protest by saying, "Unless I wash you, you have no part with me" (13:8b). There is something crucial about allowing Jesus to wash feet that appears to connect with what the cross accomplishes.

But there's even more to the footwashing than this. After washing the feet of all the disciples, Jesus adds a second level of significance: "Now that I, your Lord and Teacher, have washed your feet, you also should wash one another's feet" (13:14). He follows this up with a command: "As I have loved you, so you must love one another" (13:34). How did he love them? By washing their feet. So, there is love wrapped up into this gesture, and it's a rather humble quality of love.

How does touch figure into this loving, humble gesture? As Jesus grasps his disciples' feet, he reverses their understanding of "proper" touch, and he redefines it. The kind of love that Jesus extends to us and that we are to extend to one another is intense enough to cross boundaries that limit proximity. It takes humility to draw close enough to grasp someone's grimy feet, invading their personal space in a way that says to them, *I love you this much—let me wash your*

---

64. Keener (*John*, 2:899) recognizes this as Johannine double entendre: "to the end" indicates both the completeness of Jesus's love and its endpoint—his death.

65. Keener, *John*, 2:902; Klink, *John*, 577; R. Brown, *John*, 566. Also significant to this understanding is how Jesus lays aside his outer clothing and takes up the towel. This mirrors language of death and resurrection used in John 10:17–18, where the good shepherd lays down his life in order to take it up again.

feet. Jesus creates a pathway when he embodies a potent sort of love that the disciples had not yet experienced, and he calls them to follow his lead. And not only do they know what this kind of love looks like; they know what it *feels* like.

Grasping the Resurrected Christ

We ended the Synoptics discussion by talking about Jesus's death. For our final Johannine scene, we will address one of his resurrection appearances. The first person to whom Jesus appears is Mary Magdalene. Arriving at the tomb, Mary is devastated to see the stone removed and Jesus's body missing. She weeps because she thinks that someone has stolen it (John 20:13). She lost Jesus once, and now it appears that she's lost him again! After she encounters angels unaware, Jesus shows up, but Mary doesn't realize that it's him; she thinks that he's the gardener. And Jesus plays along: "Woman, why are you crying? Who is it you are looking for?" (20:15a). I wonder if he took delight in visiting people after his resurrection—like how it feels to surprise someone with a gift that you know they'll love. Mary says to the incognito Jesus, "If you have carried him away, tell me where you have put him" (20:15b).

Well, once Jesus says her name, "Mary," she knows it's him: "Rabboni!" *Teacher!* (20:16). Then, Jesus says a curious thing: "Do not hold on to me, for I have not yet ascended to the Father" (20:17). What does *that* mean? Many suppose that Mary has grabbed hold of Jesus: either she has swept him up into a giant hug or she has fallen prostrate at his feet, grasping onto them for dear life. Either way, she's not about to lose him again! It's also possible that her grasp and Jesus's response suggest that Mary is thinking, *Yes! Now that we have our Teacher back, things can go back to the way they were before.* But as we know, Jesus has bigger plans. From here he commissions her to go and tell the other disciples that he is alive.

Notice how touch functions differently here than in all the earlier scenes. Mary has to *let go* of Jesus in order to carry out his commission. We probably can relate to the idea of letting go of something in order to move forward or change direction. In many ways, Mary's instinct to hang on to Jesus is right on. She knows who he is, and she wants to remain as close to him as she can. All this time the Word made flesh has been drawing near to humanity—anointing eyes and washing feet—but here is where things change. Now, starting with Mary, Jesus's disciples must let go of his embodied presence and carry out this very same kind of humble, up-close, compassionate love: the church is meant to provide embodied testimony to the risen Christ.

Touch for the Earliest Readers

This chapter has suggested that rules about touch are embedded as well-worn grooves into the collective brain of every culture. Paul's proclamation that the church is one in Christ—"neither Jew nor Gentile, neither slave nor free, nor . . . male and female" (Gal. 3:28)—was a radical vision to be carried out in embodied relationship. This would have involved crossing tactile boundaries. Think about house-church gatherings: servants sharing the eucharistic meal side by side with their masters, patrons laying on hands to pray over clients, and vice versa, *greeting one another with a holy kiss.* Men, women, and children, together in proximity.

For the earliest readers, a teacher washing his students' feet was a new, uncommon practice. Touching a leper or a hemorrhaging woman to generate cleansing? That is the *opposite* of what early readers would have been conditioned to think is appropriate. Ancient readers encountering these tactile disruptions would have instinctually known these interruptions in their bodies.

These Gospel scenes display Jesus's words and deeds, and they are laced with new tactile grooves pioneered by Jesus's embodiment of love. This is what love *feels* like. It's Jesus, boldly initiating and receiving the touch of the ritually impure and socially marginalized. To weary men and women traversing a wasteland of isolation, Jesus says with his hands, *I see you. You matter.* Love feels like Mary pouring valuable perfume on her Lord's feet and taking her softest, most luxurious asset—her hair—to wipe it off. Love feels like Jesus breaking all social protocols and humbly stooping over his best friends' grimy feet with a basin of water and a towel. Ancient readers consumed words that reshaped how touch articulates love. But words can accomplish only so much. At some point they needed to transcend the page and become embodied action.

Touch for Modern Readers

Today, the general principle holds that nurturing touch is important for human flourishing. But "nurturing" touch depends on context. What one might consider comforting, another might experience as invasive. Recent movements like #MeToo have awakened and reminded the broader public of the various ways traumatic touch has (for millennia) been used to dominate, manipulate, and exert power over others. Now we are learning how to exercise greater care about what we suggest qualifies as nurturing. For those who experience skin hunger, your gentle hand on their arm in casual conversation might land as a balm to their souls. Those who are averse to touch will be relieved when you abstain from enveloping them in a hug. For both types of people, touch is precious and is to be wielded with sensitivity. For this reason, we all must exercise discernment in how we love one another.

Since skin is such a common, direct medium by which we navigate our world, we are constantly engaging touch. This makes tactile contact common and vulnerable *at the same time.* I'd like to conclude this chapter by affirming the goodness of touch as it plays out in the Gospels. As we've imagined our way through Jesus's tactile interactions, let's consider how he is not afraid to extend his hand to untouchable kinds of people. He is not worried about breaking tactile rules or being canceled by the authorities. What he *is* concerned about is the person in front of him. To each one he generously offers compassion and dignity, engaging them in tactile ways that speak their language, sensitive to their needs and loving them with unflinching wholeheartedness that says, *I care about you, and I am fully present with you right now.* Those who receive his touch *know* that he is telling the truth. They feel it.

As we read the Gospels and think about how tactile contact operates in our own world, let me encourage you to consider how you might cultivate the sense of touch in your own rhythms. Helen Keller provides extended reflection on the beauty of a cultivated sense of touch, crediting her lack of sight with this heightened awareness:

> Touch brings the blind many sweet certainties which our more fortunate fellows miss, because their sense of touch is uncultivated. When they look at things, they put their hands in their pockets. No doubt that is one reason why their knowledge is often so vague, inaccurate, and useless. . . .
>
> There is nothing, however, misty or uncertain about what we can touch. I know the faces of friends, the illimitable variety of straight and curved lines, all surfaces, the exuberance of the soil, the delicate shapes of flowers, the noble forms of trees and the range of mighty winds. Besides objects, surfaces, and atmospheric changes, I perceive countless vibrations.[66]

Certainly, there is much we can do to both increase our awareness and cultivate our experience of touch. May you enjoy what you learn as you feel your way through the Gospels going forward!

TACTILE
TRUTHS

1. The quote above from Helen Keller reflects on how a lack of sight can help cultivate the sense of touch in our world. What would it look like for you to temporarily mute one of your other senses in a way that brings out tactile experience? For this exercise, cover your eyes (such as with a sleep mask) in order to focus on the sense of touch. Here is one idea:

   a. Collect a variety of objects to explore. This could include flowers, leaves, books, a slice of bread, a soft blanket, a furry pet, a knit sweater. Describe these objects only by touch.

66. Keller, *The World I Live In*, 49–50.

   b. After this, reflect on how God fashioned the world for our tactile
   enjoyment. What can we learn about how touch can help us
   navigate our world with gratitude and wonder?

2. We often think of our worship in musical terms. What would it look
   like for you to respond to God's love in worship through a tactile-
   focused expression? Engage in an activity using touch, creating
   space to reflect on and respond to him. You could do something
   crafty or artistic, such as sketching an object with pencils or paint-
   ing with watercolor (you don't actually have to *be* artistic to do
   this). You could spend time in the dirt—planting flowers, pulling
   weeds, tilling soil. If you are near a body of water, you could take
   a walk and collect unique shells or try your hand at skipping rocks
   across still water. The point is to engage in a tactile activity so as
   to provoke reflection and communion with Christ.

8

Sensing Jesus Together

Concluding Thoughts

Thunk...thunk...thunk... As late-night hot loaves of raisin bread were knocked out of their baking pans onto the metal table, I picked up each one and plunked it onto the rack—*thunk*. I could manage one loaf, sometimes two at a time—*thunk-thunk*. Rotating my body between table and rack, I went table-rack-*thunk*, table-rack-*thunk*, over and over until all the bread—the raisin, the white, the sourdough, the wheat—was knocked out of every pan coming from the oven.

I was eighteen and newly graduated from high school when I began giving my summers to "the bakery," my family's business, which served all varieties of bread to local restaurants.[1] I was eager to earn cash to cover my college tuition and begin saving for a car, so when they put me on the swing shift with frequent overtime, I was grateful for the paycheck. But the job was not for the faint of heart.

I often worked alongside the only other female on the factory floor, Diane, whom I'd known since I was a little girl. I fancied myself at

1. Formally it was called Roma Bakery, serving the greater San Jose Bay Area since 1907 and finally shutting its doors in the wake of COVID-19. Apparently, good things can come to an end.

least as tough as Diane, and thought I could even rival my burly male cousins who worked the ovens. Once I even took a bet that I couldn't last an hour on the oven "throwing pan bread," as they called it.[2] I won the bet but only ever worked that one hour (too many burns on my forearms!). After that I felt I had proven my grit and was content to stand at the bread bin, feeding newly sliced bread onto the conveyer belt to be bagged. Some nights at the bakery, the circular lines forming my fingerprint would be sandpapered smooth (and raw) by handling hundreds of seeded loaves of bread. On other nights, the tops of my hands bore the brunt of crusty sourdough loaves zooming toward me through the slicer.

I gained new respect for the men (and Diane) who worked long, sweltering, grueling hours on this beloved factory floor, year after year. Before that, I had romanticized the bakery, which gave off yummy bready fragrances that wafted down Almaden Avenue. You smelled it before you saw the landmark white building with its enormous flour tower. However, coming face-to-face with the sweaty monotony of table-rack-*thunk*, table-rack-*thunk*—for hours upon hours—stripped me of all sentimentality about working there. It was *hard*.

Most afternoons I felt the creep of dread rising as I watched the clock tick down to the start of my 4:00 p.m. shift, never knowing if I'd get off at midnight, or 1:00 a.m., or 2:00 a.m. San Jose summers in a factory without air conditioning were pretty toasty. At sundown the giant fans cooling off the bread dried my sweaty skin but didn't remove the caked-on bits of dough, flecks of bread crusts, and dustings of flour. The later nighttime hours were especially solitary and lonely. Everyone ran out of things to say on an interminable assembly line. In those prepodcast, pre-AirPods days (ancient, I know), we contented ourselves with the boom box blaring the local hard-rock station. I took solace in my nightly Super Big Gulp of Diet Coke alongside whatever type of bread I decided to make my dinner.

Raisin bread night—what I described above—came around only once a week at the bakery, and it was my *favorite*. Inevitably there

---

2. This was the person pulling the pans from the ovens and knocking the loaves out, four and five loaves at a time. In the opening story it was a cousin pulling the pans, while I transferred the loaves to a rack.

was a loaf or two that came out misshapen and therefore unsellable, so these were set aside. We broke them apart just like I imagine Jesus would have done with the bread at the Last Supper. As we passed the loaves around, each of us would scoop out giant handfuls of the hot, steamy, raisiny middle. It was a bright spot in my solitary, repetitive workweek.

Sensory Entanglements

As we have reached the end of our multisensory tour of the Gospels, perhaps you are wondering why I've shared this slice of my past as I attempt to "tie a bow" on our study. Well, for one thing, perhaps you noticed its sensory qualities. Were you able to detect the tastes, sights, sounds, smells, and touches? Do you find your senses more attuned to the sensory aspects of a narrative than when you began? I hope so.

However, perhaps you're wondering what this story has to do with engaging Jesus with our senses. Everything, as it turns out. What I haven't shared is how that nightly grind in the monotonous, sweltering bakehouse was an absolutely formative season for me. Here is where engaging Jesus with my senses looked like more than engaging a text; this, rather, was an exercise in attentiveness to the living Word in the embodied moment. It was *sensing Jesus*.

It was in the eighth, the tenth, the eleventh hours of work, during the exhausting late hours of the night, while thunking bread onto racks and conveyer belts, that I learned that I didn't need to succumb to loneliness, because I wasn't alone. The rote quality of those summer shifts at the bakery trained my mind and spirit to wander, to meditate on Scripture, to reflect, to dream, to pray. There were moments when I languished and longed for that last hour of work, but these were often the very same moments when I just *knew* that Jesus was near—when I could see him at work and call out to him, when I listened for the shepherd's voice, and when I knew that he was listening to me.

Sensing Jesus involves the living Word speaking up to guide and encourage, while whatever happens to be going on in your sensory world attaches onto these insights. It's like high-fiving a palm branch while the living Word reminds you that you're surrounded by a great cloud of witnesses. It's handling hot, steamy bread while reflecting on provision and presence in solitary settings. All of these become entangled together to form memorable moments, carrying you through to future seasons of life.

In the early chapters of this book, I made the case that we should pay attention to our sensory lives because it is an important way we can cultivate gratitude for the goodness of this multisensory life that God has fashioned for us. But as we know, this good, sensory life does not consist only of soft kittens, lavish banquets, and masterful symphonies. Sometimes our most profoundly spiritual moments are born in the midst of sensory dissonance and discomfort. Connecting with Jesus can occur when we are at our sweatiest, at the peak of boredom and loneliness, and when we are in many ways deprived of sensory pleasantries.

In fact, many of our sensory engagements are downright traumatic, dark, and painful, the result of living in this fallen, broken world. As we have discussed, memories of these experiences become embedded into our bodies, with potent effects. These are so powerful that we often have to pivot in our plans. Quite often they are disruptive enough to cause the death of a dream. And yet Scripture suggests that God still moves in and through even these shadowy, twisted pathways. We can't always see it, and even if we do, it is often not until we look back over a long trajectory of time.

Sometimes—maybe even *most* of the time—life consists of symphonies alongside violence; it is blandness alongside scrumptious tastes, pain alongside beauty, comfort alongside suffering. Life with God is raw fingertips and delicious raisin bread on the same night. We can sense Jesus in the monotonous assembly line just like we can sense him in the stunning harmonies sung by angelic voices. Sensing Jesus happens in intricate fashion, everything entwined together: a cacophony of hard and beautiful sensory experiences.

Along with the entanglement of the good with the difficult, throughout this book we have also explored how we live in a world filled with a diversity of configurations of sensory abilities. These diversities span across individuals, communities, cultures, and centuries.

Within these collections of sensory abilities, we are reminded of the hardship, and we have especially glimpsed the potential for goodness that this sensory life has to offer. Each of us can proverbially "taste and see" that the Lord is good, using whatever sensory configurations we've been given.

Frederick Buechner once penned an invitation that fits with the aim to grow awareness of our sensory surroundings and their implications: "Listen to your life. See it for the fathomless mystery that it is. In the boredom and pain of it no less than in the excitement and gladness: touch, taste, smell your way to the holy and hidden heart of it because in the last analysis all moments are key moments, and life itself is grace."[3] As we count down to the final paragraphs of this book, let's recount the collection of insights gathered across the five senses.

Engaging the Gospels with All Our Senses

We have established that we are *sensory* beings living *sensory* lives engaging texts that narrate *sensory* worlds. In the final analysis, perhaps you'll conclude that all we've done is provide a more *sensory* version of a historical-critical approach to the text. We talked about this in chapter 2, where I admitted as much, saying that "this approach [to the Gospels] is not much different than when we read the text to understand its original historical context." It's essentially an amplified descriptive endeavor.

At the very least, I hope that this has helped you utilize your imagination alongside a heightened awareness of your physical senses, to burrow yourself more fully into the world of the text. Are you better able to grasp what Jesus's world looked like, sounded like, smelled like, tasted like, and felt like? This is valuable for how it adds color to the biblical world, kind of like putting on 3D glasses or taking a walk in a narrative character's first-century sandals. Before we move on to discuss several specific outcomes of our study, let's view the collection of sensory insights that our study has produced.

3. Buechner, *Listening to Your Life*, 2.

Our venture into the sensory world of the Gospels has provided us a multisensory portrayal of what the kingdom of God is like. These depictions consist of Jesus's interactions with others. The kingdom of God is like an extravagant dinner party—such as a wedding feast— where celebrants enjoy the finest of food and drink. As the host, Jesus welcomes everyone, regardless of race or ethnicity, economic status, gender, ability, or past actions. What matters is whether you accept his invitation and are prepared to take a seat at his side, enjoying fellowship with all who are present.

In the Gospels, the coming of the kingdom of God is marked by Jesus restoring sight, hearing, and speech to those who suffer in their lack. What a gift to gain or regain these abilities! And it is especially sweet for those living in contexts where these senses are essential for participation and acceptance in their communities.

The high rank of sight and hearing make these senses especially popular metaphors for faith. To believe is to truly see, and yet Christians are also familiar with Paul's opposite valuation of sight: we walk *by faith*, not *by sight*. This challenges us not to depend so much on our own abilities that we hamper faith and hold God at arm's length. To believe is also to have ears to hear. As sheep, believers are invited to listen for Jesus-the-good-shepherd's voice calling us by name. Hearing Jesus means engaging the Word of God and receiving encouragement. We do this when we audibly listen to someone speak Jesus's words, but we also "hear" through our other senses, like when we hear Jesus's instructions to love one another and proceed to humbly wash feet.

One of the themes that materializes again and again is dependence on Jesus. When Jesus says, "I am the bread of life," he is postured as the manna from heaven that nourishes believers unto eternity. Jesus suggests that just as our bodies require food to nourish us day by day, the ideal posture for believers is ever-dependence on him. This runs contrary to our modern context, which champions independence and autonomy. Dependence also flows through the shepherd metaphor. As sheep are invited to listen, follow, and stay near, notice how this dependence is connected to their freedom. Sheep are not truly free to enjoy nourishment and protection unless they are fully relying on the shepherd. As in our daily reliance on Jesus as living bread, sheep never outgrow their dependence. Jesus's nourishing presence and proximity are the goal. These are the beginning, middle, and end points of faith.

Smells are everywhere and nowhere in the Gospels. They are everywhere because they are woven into the fabric of daily life. They drift around the banquet table, into worship settings, and through burials of loved ones. And yet they are nowhere because the Gospel writers hardly mention them. We can relate to this dynamic because smells waft through every moment of our lives, present even when ignored. Notably, Jesus commands life out of the stench of death, and then he himself is anointed by strong fragrances for his own life-producing death and burial. How can smells bring us into conversation with God? Since scents embed themselves deep into our memories, some smells provoke anger, anxiety, or dread, while others call forth nostalgia or gratitude. What does it look like to remain attentive to and reflective about the goodness of this fragrant life we live?

Finally, we addressed how significant touch is for human flourishing, and yet its potency requires that we wield it with the utmost of care, caution, and sensitivity. Jesus healed many through the medium of touch, which often crossed ritual purity lines and ruffled feathers. The touch of Jesus provides an example of how to articulate his Father's love to others. In many ways it forged new paths and redefined the rules for what love looks like and feels like. What is the character of this love? It's a love that gets right up close to those whom society deems untouchable and lays a hand on their eyes, or ears, saying, *I see you. I am here with you. You matter.* Jesus did not correct women for breaking alabaster jars and anointing his feet. Instead, he welcomed them, even riffing on these gestures by grasping his friends' feet to wash them. By this he demonstrates compassion, saying, *Friends, this is how you love one another.*

Jesus, the Word made flesh, lived an embodied life. He engaged in sensate ways with the world and community around him. It was through these interactions that he conveyed his heart. As sensory readers engaging the Gospels, may we continue to marvel at how powerfully Jesus's words and actions articulate the heart of his Father and the dawn of the kingdom.

Reading with All Our Senses Intact

One of the unique outcomes that I hope this study has achieved is to give us permission to openly bring our embodiment into our reading of the text. In other words, rather than bracket out our sensory lives, I've encouraged us to be aware of our sensory experiences as we engage with the Gospel narratives. It's the reminder that if you've ever tasted a really fine wine, then you can imagine—because you know in your taste buds—what it might have been like to witness Jesus providing the best wine at a wedding. It gives you embodied knowledge of the goodness of the kingdom of God in Jesus.

It means that as we observe Jesus using the sense of touch to lay his hands on the sick, we are invited to consider whether our hands might convey love—and by extension, Christ's love—with potent effects. Would our prayers for those who are sick or in despair carry greater potency and compassion if we were to ask permission to lay a hand on a shoulder or to grasp a hand? Or, if you have ever smelled the stench of death or witnessed death's absolute stillness, how does this help you imagine Lazarus, or the widow's son, or Jesus himself showing signs of life in the wake of death's quiet permanence?

You may be thinking that this study brings only greater descriptive color to the narrative and no more. And maybe that's enough. But let's not forget that the Gospels claim to be more than narrative accounts describing historical events in theological terms. With that, let's move to discuss the second contribution that a sensory reading makes.

Living Gospel Texts

As we outlined in chapter 2, the Gospels consist of more than narrative content to be mined for historical insight, and they are more than narratives with theological aims. The Gospels are meant to be engaged as scriptural texts with formative purpose. That is, we are invited to engage the Gospels as living words—God's Word—given to believers for all time. As such, the Gospels invite us to engage with Jesus himself.

Think back to the hours before Jesus is arrested. John narrates a discussion that Jesus has with his friends, offering them final instructions and reassurances.[4] Here Jesus tells them that he is departing to go to the Father. The disciples find this quite troubling (understandably so!), and Jesus assures them that although he will be physically absent, they won't be alone. Jesus then discloses that the Father is sending them "another advocate" (or "paraclete"), the Spirit of truth, to be with and in them forever (14:16–17; 16:13). The Spirit will serve as their advocate, whispering wisdom into their ears and providing guidance at just the right moments. By the Spirit they will know the presence of Jesus.

Curiously, it is right in the middle of these instructions about the abiding Holy Spirit that Jesus presents another metaphor, claiming, "I am the true vine," and describing his disciples as the branches (15:1–8).[5] This beautiful image positions the disciples about as close as anyone can get to Jesus, inviting readers to imagine this sinewy union between branches and vine.

This vineyard scene alongside the loyal presence of the Advocate sets the stage for Jesus's high-priestly prayer, which reminds us that *all* who call themselves disciples of Jesus can imagine themselves as branches on the vine, listening for the shepherd's voice, eating the living manna, and enjoying the grand banquet. This is because Jesus prays not only for his disciples present with him but also for all disciples to come: "My prayer is not for them alone. I pray also for those who will believe in me through their message. . . . I have given them the glory that you gave me, that they may be one as we are one—I in them and you in me—so that they may be brought to complete unity" (17:20–23).

Jesus invites everyone who engages with these words to respond to him. What will this look like? Is his invitation compelling? Will we believe and entrust ourselves to him? If not, why not? Part of the reason a sensory approach is significant is that it brings a more

4. Often referred to as the Farewell Discourse, this is commonly viewed as beginning in John 13 (with the footwashing) and extending through the high-priestly prayer in John 17.

5. This is tied back to Old Testament imagery where Israel is presented as a vine or a vineyard (Ps. 80:8–16; Isa. 5:1–7; 27:2–6; Jer. 2:21; Ezek. 15:1–8; 17:5–10; 19:10–14; Hosea 10:1–2). In many of these portrayals, Israel has failed to remain obedient to Yahweh and thus resembles a vine failing to bear fruit or bearing bad fruit. Thus, here, Jesus is the *true* vine, fulfilling what Israel could not.

embodied quality of the narrative into view, and this has the potential to carry into the outworking of our actual embodied, sensory lives. Are we convinced that God is as good and loving as his Word says? What do we imagine that this goodness feels like? Maybe it's warm like the dawning sun or as beautiful as the sound of a loved one calling you by name. Maybe love feels like someone initiating a hearty hug, or maybe for you it's the opposite: no touch at all but simply the offer of some well-chosen words.

A sensory portrait of the Living Word gifts us with a depiction of an embodied Jesus filled to the brim with compassion. His smiling, welcoming countenance holds space for the young and the old, the sick and the healthy, the abled and the disabled, the believing and the cynical. His healing touch signals the coming kingdom, while its proximity confers dignity on the downtrodden. His ongoing presence has the power to embolden our actions with justice and to temper our words with kindness. We are invited to let our feet be washed, and then we are empowered to go and do likewise. Sensory insight into the Gospels reminds us that these texts present us with more than words to ponder: they narrate actions to embody. More than containing ethical instructions to pass along, the Gospels model how to invest in life-giving relationship.

Sensing Jesus Together

Many years ago, my husband and I participated in a local church community whose worship service gave celebratory attention to the practice of collecting tithes and offerings. Every week, when it was time to pass the plate (or the bucket, in our case), the worship leader proclaimed rather joyfully, "Church, it's time to give!" And then everyone broke out into thunderous applause and cheering. The first time this happened, it completely startled me. *What in the world is happening?* I thought. Then the second, third, and fourth times it happened, it prompted me to reflect on how joyous it actually is to offer the firstfruits of our financial resources to God in worship. Up to this point in my life, I had been accustomed to the obligatory prayer and special song that facilitated a rather low-key passing of the plate.

It didn't attract much attention, because (in my view) inviting people to give money is rather awkward. But introducing the offering with boisterous applause? That communicates something very different. It's a privilege and a joy to give back to the Lord. Practices like these have the power to reshape a community's heart.

Throughout this book I have been careful to discuss how the senses operate in both communal and individual practice. However, I am very aware that the various personal examples I've provided might skew us to focus more on individualized sensory experience. Part of this was intentional: many of us need greater awareness of how much our senses figure into daily life and into our reading. But I would be remiss if I did not underline the integral connection between these individualized insights and how they spill out into our communities. Communities are made up of individuals, after all, and individual people participate in communities based on personal conviction. These convictions, in turn, often spark entire communal movements (for good and for ill).

So how do our personal *and* communal sensory convictions encourage us to sense Jesus together? How might sensing Jesus *together* contribute to the vibrancy of God's church as we more fully embody Jesus's love? Perhaps this is something that communities discern and act on collectively. This happens when churches decide to clap and cheer when it's time to collect the offering. It happens in our eucharistic rhythms as we carry on a sensory tradition begun by Jesus himself, eating the bread and drinking from the cup *together*, in sorrow for sin and gratitude for resurrected life.

Sensing Jesus together happens when we act to alleviate the pain of the sick and the suffering of our most vulnerable. It happens when we actively seek to right the injustices encountered in this world. We sense Jesus together when we use our eyes and ears to detect those in need and when we open wide the doors of our churches and homes to neighbors we don't yet know. It happens around shared, fragrant meals with smiling, compassionate eyes; with bold, heartfelt prayers; with strong handshakes; and with generous encouragement.

Sensing Jesus is a communal endeavor just as much as it is an individualized one. Sensing Jesus together helps us align with God's Edenic design for human flourishing, cultivating life and articulating his love to one another. My hope is that together we will not squander a single minute, sensing every last drop of this life God has provided.

Conclusion

The first Johannine Epistle, closely related to John's Gospel, opens with a sensory prologue that perhaps cements for us the power of a sensory gospel. The Johannine author writes that Jesus is the one "which we have heard, which we have seen with our eyes, which we have looked at and our hands have touched—this we proclaim concerning the Word of life" (1 John 1:1). Speaking on behalf of all those who saw and heard and testified to Jesus's life, the epistle articulates the hope that all readers might have fellowship with the Father, the Son, and his church (1:2–3).

I hope that we the church, as recipients of the absent-but-present Jesus and the testimony of his disciples, can follow their lead of living into and cultivating the same quality of fellowship with the Father, Son, and Spirit that we read about in the pages of Scripture. Let's commit to do more than read the words; let's see, hear, smell, taste, and touch them. Let's do more than read *about* Jesus; let's reach out and sense him.

Bibliography

Aldrete, Gregory. "Urban Sensations: Opulence and Ordure." In *A Cultural History of the Senses in Antiquity*, edited by Jerry Toner, 45–67. Cultural History of the Senses 1. London: Bloomsbury Academic, 2019.

Arel, Stephanie N. *Affect Theory, Shame, and Christian Formation*. Cham: Palgrave Macmillan, 2016.

Aristotle. *On the Soul. Parva Naturalia. On Breath*. Translated by W. S. Hett. Loeb Classical Library 288. Cambridge: Harvard University Press, 1957.

Attridge, Harold W. "Making Scents of Paul: The Background and Sense of 2 Cor. 2:14–17." In *Early Christianity and Classical Culture: Comparative Studies in Honor of Abraham J. Malherbe*, edited by John T. Fitzgerald, Thomas H. Olbricht, and L. Michael White, 71–88. Supplements to Novum Testamentum 110. Leiden: Brill, 2003.

Austin, J. L. *Sense and Sensibilia*. New York: Oxford University Press, 1964.

Avrahami, Yael. *The Senses of Scripture: Sensory Perception in the Hebrew Bible*. Library of Biblical Studies. New York: T&T Clark, 2012.

Bailey, Kenneth. *The Good Shepherd: A Thousand-Year Journey from Psalm 23 to the New Testament*. Downers Grove, IL: IVP Academic, 2014.

Barsalou, Lawrence W. "Grounded Cognition: Past, Present, and Future." *Annual Review of Psychology* 59 (2008): 617–45.

———. "Perceptual Symbol Systems." *Behavioral and Brain Sciences* 22, no. 4 (August 1999): 577–660.

Beavis, Mary Ann. "From the Margin to the Way: A Feminist Reading of the Story of Bartimaeus." *Journal for the Feminist Study of Religion* 14, no. 1 (1998): 19–39.

———. *Mark*. Paideia. Grand Rapids: Baker Academic, 2011.

Bergen, Benjamin. *Louder Than Words: The New Science of How the Mind Makes Meaning*. New York: Basic Books, 2012.

Bergson, Henri. *Matter and Memory*. Translated by Nancy Margaret Paul and W. Scott Palmer. London: G. Allen; New York: Macmillan, 1912.

Brown, Raymond E. *The Gospel according to John (XIII–XXI): Introduction, Translation, and Notes*. Anchor Bible 29A. Garden City, NY: Doubleday, 1970.

Brown, Sherri. "Jesus in Word and Deed through the Ritual Activity of Tabernacles in John 7:1–10:21." In *Johannine Christology*, edited by Stanley E. Porter and Andrew W. Pitts, 239–59. Johannine Studies 3. Leiden: Brill, 2020.

Buechner, Frederick. *Listening to Your Life: Daily Meditations with Frederick Buechner*. San Francisco: HarperSanFrancisco, 1992.

Bull, Michael, and Les Back, eds. *The Auditory Culture Reader*. Sensory Formations Series. Oxford: Berg, 2003.

Bultmann, Rudolf. *The Gospel of John: A Commentary*. Edited by R. W. N. Hoare and J. K. Riches. Translated by G. R. Beasley-Murray. Philadelphia: Westminster, 1971.

Campbell, Constantine, and Jonathan Pennington. *Reading the New Testament as Christian Scripture: A Literary, Canonical, and Theological Survey*. Grand Rapids: Baker Academic, 2020.

Carroll, John T. *Luke: A Commentary*. New Testament Library. Louisville: Westminster John Knox, 2012.

Carson, D. A. *The Gospel According to John*. Pillar New Testament Commentary. Grand Rapids: Eerdmans, 1991.

Carson, D. A., Douglas Moo, and Leon Morris. *An Introduction to the New Testament*. Grand Rapids: Zondervan, 1992.

Chen, Diane. *Luke*. New Covenant Commentary Series. Eugene, OR: Cascade Books, 2017.

Clark-Soles, Jaime. *Reading John for Dear Life: A Spiritual Walk with the Fourth Gospel*. Louisville: Westminster John Knox, 2016.

Classen, Constance. "The Breath of God: Sacred Histories of Scent." In *The Smell Culture Reader*, edited by Jim Drobnick, 375–90. Oxford: Berg, 2006.

————. *The Deepest Sense: A Cultural History of Touch*. Urbana: University of Illinois Press, 2012.

————. "Fingertips: Writing about Touch." In *The Book of Touch*, edited by Constance Classen, 1–12. Oxford: Berg, 2005.

————. "Foundations for an Anthropology of the Senses." *International Social Science Journal* 49, no. 153 (1997): 401–12.

————. "McLuhan in the Rainforest." In *Empire of the Senses: The Sensual Culture Reader*, edited by David Howes, 147–63. Oxford: Berg, 2005.

————. "The Witch's Senses." In *Empire of the Senses: The Sensual Culture Reader*, edited by David Howes, 70–84. Oxford: Berg, 2005.

————. *Worlds of Sense: Exploring the Senses in History and across Cultures*. London: Routledge, 1993.

Classen, Constance, David Howes, and Anthony Synnott. *Aroma: The Cultural History of Smell*. London: Routledge, 1994.

Coakley, J. F. "The Anointing at Bethany and the Priority of John." *Journal of Biblical Literature* 107, no. 2 (June 1988): 241–56.

Cosgrove, Charles. "A Woman's Unbound Hair in the Greco-Roman World, with Special Reference to the Story of the 'Sinful Woman' in Luke 7:36–50." *Journal of Biblical Literature* 124, no. 4 (2005): 675–92.

Davies, W. D., and Dale Allison Jr. *A Critical and Exegetical Commentary on the Gospel according to Saint Matthew*, vol. 1, *Introduction and Commentary on Matthew I–VII*. International Critical Commentary. Edinburgh: T&T Clark, 1988.

Douglass, Frederick. *My Bondage and My Freedom*. Edited by James M'Cune Smith. New York: Miller, Ortan & Mulligan, 1855.

Edwards, James. *The Gospel according to Luke*. Pillar New Testament Commentary. Grand Rapids: Eerdmans, 2015.

Elvey, Anne F. *The Matter of the Text: Material Engagements between Luke and the Five Senses*. Bible in the Modern World 37. Sheffield: Sheffield Phoenix, 2011.

Evans, Craig. *Mark 8:27–16:20*. Word Biblical Commentary 34B. Grand Rapids: Zondervan, 2018.

————. *Matthew*. New Cambridge Bible Commentary. Cambridge: Cambridge University Press, 2012.

Finnegan, Ruth. "Tactile Communication." In *The Book of Touch*, edited by Constance Classen, 18–25. Oxford: Berg, 2005.

Forger, Deborah. "Jesus as God's Word(s): Aurality, Epistemology and Embodiment in the Gospel of John." *Journal for the Study of the New Testament* 42, no. 3 (2020): 274–302.

Fox, Bethany McKinney. *Disability and the Way of Jesus: Holistic Healing in the Gospels and the Church*. Downers Grove, IL: InterVarsity, 2019.

Gibbs, Raymond, Jr. *Embodiment and Cognitive Science*. Cambridge: Cambridge University Press, 2006.

Goldworm, Dawn, and Venkatesh Murthy. "Olfaction in Science and Society." Public lecture, moderated by Catherine Dulac. *Harvard Museum of Natural History YouTube Channel*, December 2020, https://www.youtube.com/watch?v=J-LQoqBQ8T4.

Gosbell, Louise. "The Woman with the 'Flow of Blood' (Mark 5:25–34)." *Journal of Gospels and Acts Research* 2 (September 2018): 22–43.

Green, Joel. *The Gospel of Luke*. New International Commentary on the New Testament. Grand Rapids: Eerdmans, 1997.

Gundry, Robert. *Mark: A Commentary on His Apology for the Cross*. Grand Rapids: Eerdmans, 1993.

Hachlili, Rachel. *Jewish Funerary Customs, Practices, and Rites in the Second Temple Period*. Supplements to the Journal for the Study of Judaism 94. Boston: Brill, 2005.

Hall, Edward T. *The Hidden Dimension*. Garden City, NY: Anchor Books, 1969.

Hamm, Dennis. "The Tamid Service in Luke-Acts: The Cultic Background behind Luke's Theology of Worship (Luke 1:5–25; 18:9–14; 24:50–53; Acts 3:1; 10:3, 30)." *Catholic Biblical Quarterly* 65, no. 2 (2003): 215–31.

Hanger, Jeannine. "The Role of Touch in Comprehending Love: Jesus's Foot Washing in John 13." *Journal for Interdisciplinary Biblical Studies* 4, no. 1 (2022): 39–60.

———. *Sensing Salvation in the Gospel of John: The Embodied, Sensory Qualities of Participation in the* I Am *Sayings*. Biblical Interpretation Series 213. Leiden: Brill, 2023.

Harvey, Susan Ashbrook. *Scenting Salvation: Ancient Christianity and the Olfactory Imagination*. Berkeley: University of California Press, 2006.

Heil, John Paul. *The Gospel of Matthew: Worship in the Kingdom of Heaven*. Cambridge: James Clarke, 2018.

Howes, David, ed. *Empire of the Senses: The Sensual Culture Reader*. Oxford: Berg, 2005.

———. Introduction to *Empire of the Senses: The Sensual Culture Reader*, edited by David Howes, 1–17. Oxford: Berg, 2005.

———. "Olfaction and Transition: An Essay on the Ritual Uses of Smell." *Canadian Review of Sociology & Anthropology* 24, no. 3 (August 1987): 398–416.

Howes, David, and Constance Classen. *Ways of Sensing: Understanding the Senses in Society*. New York: Routledge, 2014.

Hull, John. *In the Beginning There Was Darkness: A Blind Person's Conversations with the Bible*. London: Bloomsbury T&T Clark, 2001.

Hylen, Susan. "The Shepherd's Risk: Thinking Metaphorically with John's Gospel." *Biblical Interpretation* 24, no. 3 (2016): 382–99.

Johnson, Mark. *The Body in the Mind: The Bodily Basis of Meaning, Imagination, and Reason*. Chicago: University of Chicago Press, 1987.

Keener, Craig. *Christobiography: Memory, History, and the Reliability of the Gospels*. Grand Rapids: Eerdmans, 2019.

———. *The Gospel of John: A Commentary*. 2 vols. Grand Rapids: Baker Academic, 2003.

Keller, Helen. *The World I Live In*. London: Hodder and Stoughton, 1908.

Klink, Edward W. *John*. Zondervan Exegetical Commentary on the New Testament. Grand Rapids: Zondervan, 2016.

Korsmeyer, Carolyn. "Introduction: Perspectives on Taste." In *The Taste Culture Reader: Experiencing Food and Drink*, edited by Carolyn Korsmeyer, 1–9. Sensory Formations. Oxford: Berg, 2005.

———. *Making Sense of Taste: Food and Philosophy*. Ithaca, NY: Cornell University Press, 2014.

Kurek-Chomycz, Dominika. "The Fragrance of Her Perfume: The Significance of Sense Imagery in John's Account of the Anointing in Bethany." *Novum Testamentum* 52, no. 4 (2010): 334–54.

Kysar, Robert. "Johannine Metaphor—Meaning and Function: A Literary Case Study of John 10:1–18." *Semeia* 53 (1991): 81–111.

Lakoff, George, and Mark Johnson. *Metaphors We Live By*. Chicago: University of Chicago Press, 1980.

Lawrence, Louise. "Exploring the Sense-scape of the Gospel of Mark." *Journal for the Study of the New Testament* 33, no. 4 (2011): 387–97.

———. *Sense and Stigma in the Gospels: Depictions of Sensory-Disabled Characters*. Oxford: Oxford University Press, 2013.

Lee, Dorothy. "The Gospel of John and the Five Senses." *Journal of Biblical Literature* 129, no. 1 (2010): 115–27.

———. "Imagery." In *How John Works: Storytelling in the Fourth Gospel*, edited by Douglas Estes and Ruth Sheridan, 151–69. Resources for Biblical Study 86. Atlanta: SBL Press, 2016.

———. *Transfiguration*. New Century Theology. London: Continuum, 2004.

Lincoln, Andrew. "The Lazarus Story: A Literary Perspective." In *The Gospel of John and Christian Theology*, edited by Richard Bauckham and Carl Mosser, 211–32. Grand Rapids: Eerdmans, 2008.

Macaskill, Grant. *Autism and the Church: Bible, Theology and Community*. Waco: Baylor University Press, 2019.

Magness, Jodi. "Ossuaries and the Burials of Jesus and James." *Journal of Biblical Literature* 124, no. 1 (2005): 121–54.

Matera, Frank. "The Prologue as the Interpretative Key to Mark's Gospel." *Journal for the Study of the New Testament* 34, no. 1 (1988): 3–20.

McLuhan, Marshall. "Inside the Five Sense Sensorium." In *Empire of the Senses: The Sensual Culture Reader*, edited by David Howes, 43–52. Oxford: Berg, 2005.

Meek, Esther L. *Loving to Know: Introducing Covenant Epistemology*. Eugene, OR: Cascade Books, 2001.

Miller, William Ian. "Darwin's Disgust." In *Empire of the Senses: The Sensual Culture Reader*, edited by David Howes, 335–54. Oxford: Berg, 2005.

Mohr, Mariana von, Louise P. Kirsch, and Aikaterini Fotopoulou. "Social Touch Deprivation during COVID-19: Effects on Psychological Wellbeing and Craving Interpersonal Touch." *Royal Society Open Science* 8, September 2021, https://royalsocietypublishing.org/doi/10.1098/rsos.210287.

Montagu, Ashley. *Touching: The Human Significance of the Skin*. New York: Harper & Row, 1986.

Ong, Walter J. *The Presence of the Word: Some Prolegomena for Cultural and Religious History*. New Haven: Yale University Press, 1967.

Osborne, Grant R. *Matthew*. Zondervan Exegetical Commentary on the New Testament. Grand Rapids: Zondervan, 2010.

Pennington, Jonathan. *The Sermon on the Mount and Human Flourishing: A Theological Commentary*. Grand Rapids: Baker Academic, 2017.

Philo. *On Abraham. On Joseph. On Moses*. Translated by F. H. Colson. Loeb Classical Library 289. Cambridge: Harvard University Press, 1935.

Potter, David. "The Social Life of the Senses." In *A Cultural History of the Senses in Antiquity*, edited by Jerry Toner, 23–44. Cultural History of the Senses 1. London: Bloomsbury Academic, 2019.

Ricoeur, Paul. "Lectures on Imagination." Lectures presented at the University of Chicago, Chicago, IL, 1975.

Roberts, Lissa. "The Death of the Sensual Chemist." In *Empire of the Senses: The Sensual Culture Reader*, edited by David Howes, 106–27. Oxford: Berg, 2005.

Sandy, D. Brent. *Hear Ye the Word of the Lord: What We Miss If We Only Read the Bible*. Downers Grove, IL: IVP Academic, 2024.

Sigley, Isobel. "It Has Touched Us All: Commentary on the Social Implications of Touch during the COVID-19 Pandemic." *Social Sciences & Humanities Open* 2 (July 24, 2020): 1–5. https://www.sciencedirect.com/science/article/pii/S2590291120300401?via%3Dihub.

Smith, Dennis E. *From Symposium to Eucharist: The Banquet in the Early Christian World*. Minneapolis: Fortress, 2003.

Smith, James K. A. *You Are What You Love: The Spiritual Power of Habit*. Grand Rapids: Brazos, 2016.

Stein, Robert H. *Mark*. Baker Exegetical Commentary on the New Testament. Grand Rapids: Baker Academic, 2013.

Stewart, Susan. "Remembering the Senses." In *Empire of the Senses: The Sensual Culture Reader*, edited by David Howes, 59–69. Oxford: Berg, 2005.

Story, J. Lyle. "All Is Now Ready: An Exegesis of 'The Great Banquet' (Luke 14:15–24) and 'The Marriage Feast' (Matthew 22:1–14)." *American Theological Inquiry* 2, no. 2 (July 2009): 67–79.

Strauss, Mark. *Mark*. Zondervan Exegetical Commentary on the New Testament. Grand Rapids: Zondervan, 2014.

Synnott, Anthony. *The Body Social: Symbolism, Self, and Society*. London: Routledge, 1993.

Taylor, George. "Ricœur's Philosophy of Imagination." *Journal of French Philosophy* 16, nos. 1–2 (Spring–Fall 2006): 93–104.

Theodore of Mopsuestia. *Commentarius in Evangelium Johannis Apostoli*. Edited by J.-M Vosté. Corpus Scriptorum Christianiorum Orientalium 115. Louvain: Ex Officina Orientali, 1940.

Thiessen, Matthew. *Jesus and the Forces of Death: The Gospels' Portrayal of Ritual Impurity within First-Century Judaism*. Grand Rapids: Baker Academic, 2020.

Thompson, Marianne Meye. *John: A Commentary*. New Testament Library. Louisville: Westminster John Knox, 2015.

———. "The Raising of Lazarus in John 11: A Theological Reading." In *The Gospel of John and Christian Theology*, edited by Richard Bauckham and Carl Mosser, 233–44. Grand Rapids: Eerdmans, 2008.

Toner, Jerry. "Introduction: Sensing the Ancient Past." In *A Cultural History of the Senses in Antiquity*, edited by Jerry Toner, 1–21. Cultural History of the Senses 1. London: Bloomsbury Academic, 2019.

Turner, David L. *Matthew*. Baker Exegetical Commentary on the New Testament. Grand Rapids: Baker Academic, 2008.

van der Kolk, Bessel. *The Body Keeps the Score: Brain, Mind, and Body in the Healing of Trauma*. New York: Penguin Books, 2014.

Vinge, Louise. *The Five Senses: Studies in a Literary Tradition*. Lund: Liber-Läromedel, 1975.

Wahlen, Clinton. "Healing." In *Dictionary of Jesus and the Gospels*, edited by Joel B. Green, Jeannine K. Brown, and Nicholas Perrin, 362–70. Downers Grove, IL: IVP Academic, 2013.

Walsh, Colleen. "What the Nose Knows." *The Harvard Gazette*, February 27, 2020, https://news.harvard.edu/gazette/story/2020/02/how-scent-emotion -and-memory-are-intertwined-and-exploited/.

Watkin, Christopher. *The Bible and Biblical Critical Theory: How the Bible's Unfolding Story Makes Sense of Modern Life and Culture*. Grand Rapids: Zondervan Academic, 2022.

Webster, Jane. *Ingesting Jesus: Eating and Drinking in the Gospel of John*. Academia Biblica 6. Leiden: Brill, 2003.

Wegner, Paul D. *Isaiah: An Introduction and Commentary*. Tyndale Old Testament Commentaries 20. Downers Grove, IL: IVP Academic, 2021.

Wilson, Brittany. "Seeing Divine Speech: Sensory Intersections in Luke's Birth Narrative and Beyond." *Journal for the Study of the New Testament* 42, no. 3 (2000): 251–73.

———. "The Smell of Sacrifice: Scenting the Christian Story in Luke-Acts." *Catholic Biblical Quarterly* 83, no. 2 (2021): 257–75.

Wright, N. T. *The Resurrection of the Son of God*. Christian Origins and the Question of God 3. Minneapolis: Fortress, 2003.

Yong, Amos. *The Bible, Disability, and the Church: A New Vision of the People of God*. Grand Rapids: Eerdmans, 2011.

———. *Theology and Down Syndrome: Reimagining Disability in Later Modernity*. Waco: Baylor University Press, 2007.

Index